Praise for the Author

"The world needs ambitious women. Amanda Blesing's work provides a thoughtful framework to help women channel their talents strategically so they can make a difference and build a powerful personal brand. That's the true path to standing out."

> - **Dorie Clark**, author of *Stand Out* and *Reinventing You*; adjunct professor, Duke University's Fuqua School of Business

"I first met Amanda as a fellow professional speaker and was impressed by her focus, discipline and passion for her topic of helping women create a career that really counts. What a treat to discover that she has an equal talent for writing, as she brings to life her humour and wisdom to question assumptions within the pages of this book!"

> - **Dr Mollie Marti**, CEO National Resilience Institute; researcher; international speaker; author; psychologist and lawyer

"This book is such a great handbook for anyone working in corporate or business who is trying to get to that next level but is just not quite sure how. If I could summarise with one key statement it would be 'get out of your own way and just get on and do what it is you need to do to make a difference in your life'. Thanks Amanda for inspiring women everywhere."

> - **Sharon Jurd**, international speaker and author of *Extraordinary Women in Franchising* and *How to Grow Your Business Faster than your Competitor*

"Amanda's insights provide a powerful roadmap for women everywhere at any stage of their career as they explore what it is to *Step Up, Speak Out and Take Charge* in their careers and communities. Amanda's unique perspective and sense of humour really help the reader to understand the power of belief, drive and action as tools for getting ahead."

> **- Emma Isaacs**, Founder/Global CEO at Business Chicks USA

"I mentored Amanda as she started to 'unpack' what it is she knew about women, career and ambition. Her own drive, determination and passion to help others was clear from the outset and her vision is really clear. I'm delighted she has taken this step in her own career journey and has written *Step Up, Speak Out, Take Charge,* a career changing book, that will help others get there too."

> **- Christina Guidotti,** author; speaker; mentor; CEO at
> Leading Women; partner at Thought Leaders Global

"If you've ever felt stuck in a career rut, or pigeon holed in a role that isn't working anymore, then *Step Up, Speak Out, Take Charge* is the book for you. Amanda's refreshing honesty and sense of humour make this an easy to read, yet a powerful guide for women wanting to fast-track their career progress."

> **- Janine Garner**, speaker; mentor and author of *From
> Me to We*

"Amanda's focus is on helping women see that a pathway to leadership is not simply a nice thing to do, but essential for business. Her quirky ability to use stories and colourful phrasing means that leadership is accessible to anyone who chooses that pathway. I especially love her explanation of The Revolutionary – 'If you can't find a seat at the table, bring your own chair!' and 'If you don't like the way things are then change them'. These are the people who make change happen and Amanda is certainly a Revolutionary Woman with a mission. Buy a copy today, read it and add your voice to the cause of overcoming the gap throughout our workforce. Even better, buy a second copy and give it to a woman who needs encouragement to reach her destiny or someone who should be giving encouragement to women."

- **Lynette Gray**, speaker and author of *Women in Workboots*

"With so much media around women breaking glass ceilings, leaning out and speaking up, there is usually still a void on practical solutions of how to strive for that next level. Amanda's straightforward approach delivers on these solutions. Her focus on mindset, getting out of your comfort zone and practical strategies mean that no matter what age, or industry, this book will definitely help you to get ahead."

- **Louise Agnew**, author, *Worthy Women, stories to inspire financial confidence and success in your life*

Step Up, Speak Out, Take Charge

GLOBAL
PUBLISHING
GROUP

Global Publishing Group
Australia • New Zealand • Singapore • America • London

Step Up, Speak Out,

Take Charge

A **woman's** **guide** to **getting** **ahead** in **your** career

Amanda Blesing

First Edition 2016

Copyright © 2016 Amanda Blesing

National Library of Australia

Cataloguing-in-Publication entry:

Creator: Blesing, Amanda, author

Title: Step Up, Speak Out, Take Charge : A Woman's Guide to Getting Ahead in Your Career / Amanda Blesing.

ISBN: 9781925288377 (paperback)

Subjects: Women - Employment.
Career development.
Women - Promotions.
Successful people - Conduct of life.

Dewey Number: 331.702082

Published by Global Publishing Group
PO Box 517 Mt Evelyn, Victoria 3796 Australia
Email info@GlobalPublishingGroup.com.au

For further information about orders:
Phone: +61 3 9739 4686 or Fax +61 3 8648 6871

Dedication

I dedicate this book to ambitious women everywhere who have the belief, drive and commitment to action to pursue a career that makes a bigger difference.

Vive la révolution!

#AmbitionRevolution #FeminineAmbition #LookOutCSuiteHereSheComes

- Amanda Blesing

Acknowledgements

Thank you to the people in my life who have inspired and supported me to get my ideas out in print:

- To my husband Russell, for listening to me endlessly and patiently, as I sounded out ideas and tested notions in the safety of the home

- To my Mum Dianne, who inspired me on a journey of lifelong learning

- To my Dad Don, who introduced me to the concept of feminism in my early teens

- To Sheryl Sandberg, who inspired millions with her *Lean In* message

- To Katty Kay and Claire Shipman who, unbeknownst to them, helped me move forward despite doubt, underestimation and a big gap in confidence

- To my mentor Christina Guidotti, who helped me bring my ideas to life and express them in ways that inspire others

- To a couple of great managers – Murray Paterson, who taught me that male leaders also aspire to more collaborative and inclusive leadership practices; and Dan Klein who taught me the value of giving and receiving feedback

- To Tara Sophia Mohr, who inspired me to play a much bigger game

- To Carol Dweck, who, without her amazing work on the growth mindset, I would not have written this book

- To Avril Henry, who helped me to see that it was indeed my time to shine

- To the men and women of the consumer affairs industry, who taught me the value of finding your *why*, empowering you to *fight the good fight* even when feeling uncertain

- To my sister Joanne, who is one of the most courageous women I know

- To my brother Paul, who inspired many stories

- To my wonderfully supportive clients, who encourage and inspire me daily, as much as I inspire them

- And to my publisher Darren Stephens and his team, who held my hand through much of the process and nurtured my budding entrepreneurial spirit

If your name isn't mentioned, it's not because you didn't help me, it's merely that there is not enough time or space to list everyone. Thank you everyone for the part you played.

Contents

FREE BONUS OFFER
Valued at $147.50

To help you create a career that makes a bigger difference more easily I've included a bonus set of interviews. During this series you will learn about different challenges faced in different industries, overcoming obstacles, negotiation strategies, the importance of coaches and mentors and much, much more.

Hear tips and traps from leading women including ...

- An Australian based marketing entrepreneur with an NED career

- An Australian based academic with a global brand and reputation

- An International decision making expert

- A USA based high performance coach who helps elite business people and athletes

- A Canadian negotiation expert with expertise in gender diversity

Check back regularly for additional bonus resources as they become available.

The
Ambiti◉n
Revolution
a m a n d a b l e s i n g . c o m

Claim your FREE bonus gift by going to

www.AmandaBlesing.com/bonuses

Introduction

"There is a stunning moment in the life of an Ambition Revolutionary when she realises that she doesn't need anyone to hold her hand, she is enough and she is on the right track with meaningful and important work to nourish her soul and create change. Have you had your stunning moment yet?" – Amanda Blesing

The Back Story

My professional background is in the association sector where for 20 years I've supported professionals to be more .... professional. One of the things I noticed while working alongside those in professional roles, was that women tended to require a different style of encouragement in order to step up into leadership roles or opportunities. I would invite women to speak and they would handball me to male colleagues, staff or their manager. I'd call for papers and 10 men would respond and only one woman. I observed as the men would leapfrog over women when it came to going for promotions and even nominating for awards. It was fascinating and not a little disheartening – and yet the women looked like they were doing great work – but frequently uncertain about navigating some of this newer terrain

Since leaving the association sector I developed a program called The Ambition Revolution – one on one mentoring for professional women – to assist them with confidence, to remain strategic, agile and focused on the bigger game

For those already leading, the program assists them to embrace and occupy expert status more easily. Alternatively, I deliver tailored programs for organisations who are trying to increase the profile of women in leadership, but struggling to do so.

In Australia women are paid on average 17% approx. less than men, and we remain heavily under-represented in C-suites and Boards. There are times the system and/or bias are to blame, situations that are clearly active discrimination and yet there are also times where we women perpetuate the cycle. Without wanting to focus on 'fixing the women', in this book I examine a range of solutions that women can put in place to address their own situation. I hope by writing this book I will inspire women to *Step Up, Speak Out and Take Charge* of their own success, and encourage men to understand that some character traits generally regarded as feminine – and therefore negative – are actually advantageous in a modern working world.

We are bound by stereotypes whether we like it or not. When we behave a certain way if it goes against the stereotype we run the risk of other people judging or criticising. We also feel uncomfortable when we behave in ways that are non-stereotypical, particularly when stressed.

From my own experiences, at times when my husband has earned more than me, no-one says a word. It's expected. But if for some reason I confide to my friends that I earn more than my husband then they all caution me to be careful who I talk about this with and that we don't want to hurt his ego. I'm lucky in my relationship that we have transparent discussions about this sort of thing and understand that it's swings and roundabouts, where sometimes I'll earn more, and sometimes he'll earn more. It's okay. But the stereotype remains that the man should ideally be earning more than the woman, hence the caution from my caring friends.

My clients frequently tell me that when offered roles, their mothers, sisters, female friends are all very proud and happy, but cautious when it comes to the negotiation of the package and encourage them 'not to rock the boat' or they might lose the role. Once again, this is clearly hitting up against a stereotyped norm, whether we like it or not.

Your career is not all about money but remuneration is one area where we can clearly measure and quantify what's working and what's not. I suggest that while it's only one area, it's a reflection of what else is going on in other areas of your career, including leadership aspirations and other ambitious goals or projects, and we can extrapolate.

My personal recommendation is that we need to understand the 'masculine' playing field so we can work it in effectively and sustainably, but maintain the 'feminine' where it really counts. After all, the gender diversity argument is predicated on this.

"Women who seek to be equal with men lack ambition."
– Timothy Leary

Vive la révolution!

#AmbitionRevolution #FeminineAmbition #LookOutCSuiteHereSheComes

Chapter 1

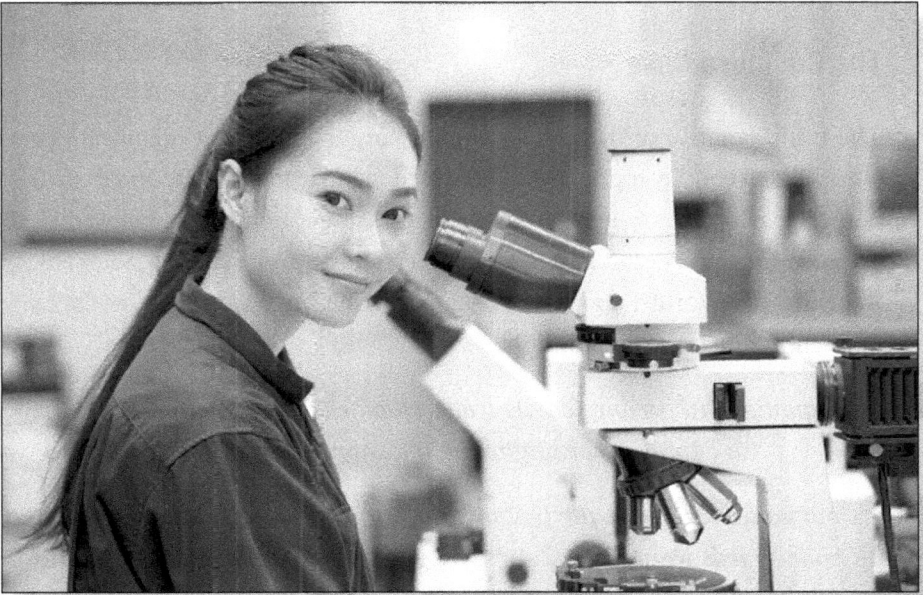

Why it's Important for Women to Embrace Ambition

Chapter 1

Why it's Important for Women to Embrace Ambition

The Business Case

The basic premise of the gender equality argument is that organisations with women equally represented in the leadership team (C-suite and Board) outperform others on a wide range of measures including profitability, productivity, risk/compliance, customer ratings and staff engagement. Recently the World Economic Forum published two powerful statistics that really illustrate the point:

"Companies with strong female leadership deliver a 36% higher return on equity, according to the index provider MSCI."

"Companies ranked in the bottom quarter in terms of gender diversity on their boards were hit by 24% more governance-related controversies than average."

– (It's official, companies with women on Boards perform better – World Economic Forum December 2015)

For specific evidence you can head over to the Workplace Gender Equality Agency site here in Australia www.wgea.gov.au, or for a more global view to www.catalyst.org.

The problem remains unsolved

Despite this overwhelming evidence, there is a crisis going on right now in the corporate sector. Gender diversity targets have been put in place and diversity measures established; yet women are either not finding the opportunities, or choosing not to take on senior leadership roles and accept traditionally defined increases in responsibility. Instead many are opting out, leaning out, and stepping sideways or down in favour of flexibility, alternative ways of working and autonomy.

A 2014 US report by Bain & Company, *Everyday Moments of Truth: Frontline managers are key to women's career opportunities* shares the idea that women are losing ambition once they get to work. Despite women being far more ambitious than men when they first arrive in a role, after only two years there is a steep decline in the number of women who are still keen for advancement.

The Australian context is similar. "Despite the fact that women comprise almost 60% of university graduates and 46% of the workforce, only 10% of senior leaders and 4% of CEOs in Australian ASX200 companies are women." (Actions Speak Louder Than Words, Bain & Co, Nov 2014) Perhaps more significantly, 60% of women don't feel they have equal opportunity to be promoted into senior roles at the same rate as their male colleagues.

Sheryl Sandberg of Facebook has put out the call for women to 'lean in' and put up their hand for big assignments – take promotions when offered, negotiate well and stop leaning out. You can learn more via her viral talk on TED.com – *'Why we have too few women leaders'*.

Katty Kay and Claire Shipman also call for action – with action being the key word and the solution. They have authored two books together on similar topics *Womenomics* and *The Confidence Code*. Their multiple references to research in the field paints a clear picture that not only do women have substantial consumer spending power, but that organisations with women in senior roles and on the Board significantly outperform organisations with few or no women occupying top roles, on a range of critical indicators of success including profitability, productivity, risk mitigation and employee satisfaction.

Additionally, their research points to a confidence gap – and that women frequently experience a lack of confidence, and that socialisation, expectation and biology are partly to blame. This gap in confidence may be a key contributor in keeping women from stepping up and remaining ambitious. Their premise is that this confidence gap keeps many women from pressing on towards the top, despite being eminently well qualified, highly skilled and extremely capable.

Knowledge is power and with power comes great responsibility to create change. There are ways to overcome this gap with programs designed specifically for women, with a deep understanding of the significant issues that many women go through as they juggle work-life balance, family and societal expectations and stereotypes while they frequently mask their own ambitions, dreams and goals in order to assist others pursue theirs.

Feminine Leadership the Way of the 21st Century

We've all seen plenty of articles about what it is that women do wrong. Sad to say, I've certainly contributed my fair share in that space. Why? Because they get higher read rates from both men and women alike and in a world where attention is a precious resource yet is squandered freely, in order to grab attention many of us frequently default to negative headlines.

But the evidence is becoming more and more clear; when there is gender diversity in the leadership team, organisations have a better track record of achieving great results including increased productivity, increased profitability, better risk mitigation, higher staff engagement and higher customer satisfaction ratings amongst other things. In fact, if I could create an 'app for that' delivering the same performance benefits as women in the C-suite, I would already be retired and focused on my charitable contributions!

The reality is somewhat more challenging, as organisations and governments struggle to meet gender diversity targets, with women hitting up against roadblocks, brick walls and glass ceilings of bias, discrimination and resistance to change.

Our business culture is saturated with images of masculine leadership as the ideal – strong, decisive, direct and to the point. Female leaders as role models are still few and far between in business and politics the world over, and women are frequently cast in roles of either the 'hard-nosed bitch' or, at the other end of the spectrum, those with one or two characteristics such as 'grace and poise'. I'm confident that while grace and poise are wonderful things, feminine leadership is made up of much, much more.

In addition, there is a tendency for us to fall back on all or nothing thinking – if one woman makes a mistake, gets something wrong or even behaves in a less than leaderly way – it becomes a transgression by all women, judged by both men and women everywhere. You might remember Julia Gillard, former Prime Minister of Australia, who tripped and fell and it was caught on camera. At the time I was travelling in the USA and this particular piece of footage was screened on a repeating loop over and over on news reels with various commentators discussing at great length the appropriateness (or lack thereof) of her footwear. Remember this was in another country and therefore entirely irrelevant, however it became a warning for all women everywhere to wear appropriate footwear or bear the consequences to their credibility. The irony of the situation remains that Gillard was wearing modest heels at the time, certainly nothing to be critiqued but perhaps more importantly, this would not have happened if she had been a man. Women heads of state and leaders are still a rare breed, so every move is scrutinised.

What exactly is it that women bring to the table that appears to add such great value? What do women do right – not wrong? What are these characteristics/traits/values? And are they limited to only women? We're focused on 'fixing the problem' but the perhaps these characteristics should instead be highly sought after by both men and women.

The Athena Doctrine by John Gerzema and Michael D'Antonio explores a range of characteristics that are traditionally seen as the domain of the feminine, are great for solving problems in business, and are also seen by younger generations of future leaders as highly desirable.

> *"Femininity is the operating system of twenty-first century progress. Women – and the men who can think like them – are creating a future we'll all want to inhabit."* – John Gezerma

Why? Because we live in a world that is increasingly global, interconnected, social, transparent and interdependent. This new world needs long term solutions, collaborative strategies and joined up thinking. These traits are more than a simple preference. In fact, it would appear they are more in the needs/must category.

The traits/skills/characteristics that operate well in this new joined up global economy include:

- Listening
- Communicating
- Collaborating
- Adapting
- Promoting a positive culture where purpose and profits co-exist
- Inclusive decision-making
- Nurturing of relationships

As you can see, anyone can do these things – men and women alike. They are not gender specific, but more traditionally aligned with *the feminine*.

Masculine leadership

Masculine leadership (not necessarily only the domain of men) is defined as something that's a top down, hierarchical and bureaucratic leadership structure, with the boss knowing where the organisation is going and everyone else following – playing their part like cogs in a machine. In fact, our military forces, police departments, judicial systems, academia, governments and many large corporates are structured around this leadership model. A masculine leadership model is sometimes more adversarial in style, which in turn promotes competition, silos and isolation.

Binary model

"There is no Mars and Venus, but in fact we are allies here on planet earth and our interests are the same."– Michael Kimmel

I acknowledge that this is a binary model. There are many ways to lead, and linking leadership styles to gender stereotypes is a narrow way of thinking which continues to reinforce and perpetuate stereotypes. The differences between the way men and other men think or lead, and the differences between the way women and other women think or lead, are probably equally as great if not greater, than the differences between the way men and women lead.

However it helps us to reflect on other options when we acknowledge alternative methods. It helps us to step into the realm of leadership more naturally when we understand that there is more than one style in which to do it. Just as we now understand, with the help of fellow revolutionary, Susan Cain, founder of *The Quiet Revolution* and author of *Quiet*, that introverts make great leaders too, it also helps those who are less adversarial and more inclusive in style, to see leadership as an option, however simply not in the traditional model.

> *"Being bold is not about being right, being perfect, or knowing it all.*
> *Rather it is about marshalling resources, information and people.*
> *It involves seeing problems as opportunities, occasionally flying by*
> *the seat of your pants, and ultimately being willing to fall flat on*
> *your face and know you will survive."*
>
> – Dr Valerie Young

Balanced voice

Balanced voice is a term I first heard entrepreneur and media personality Naomi Simson use. She drew attention to the overuse of quotes by men in literature, leadership and success narratives. While men do achieve things, so too do women. It's simply that women's endeavours haven't been as catalogued as much as men's endeavours. Because of this, I've chosen to do my part in restoring the balance by predominantly featuring quotes by women.

It's the same with leadership role models. If all we ever see, read about or hear about are masculine role models, we keep reinforcing the stereotypes, and fewer women will see leadership of business, government or community as viable or desirable options. Nor will others consider women as viable leadership candidates as they will still represent an unknown, untested entity.

> *"Only 11% of top business school case studies have a female*
> *protagonist."*
>
> – Lesley Symons, *Harvard Business Review*

Recently the *Harvard Business Review* published an article in which many business schools and universities had allowed their materials to be audited for gender bias. They discovered that the dial hasn't moved much in terms of reinforcing stereotypes about leadership. Most of the content in texts books and case studies (and, according to my own sources, lecturers in MBA programs) are still male and I suspect white and middle aged as well. While some concerted effort is being made, and there is a commitment by universities to change, until there is some element of transparency, reporting against a standard, or performance measurement against KPIs with a sting in the tail, things simply won't change.

Leadership within your grasp

Reading about alternative models of leadership will help you see that leadership is indeed within your grasp – where previously you might have considered your style not strong or direct enough.

So, as you do the work in preparing yourself for you next jaunt or dabble into leadership (whether that's people leadership, project leadership, thought leadership or personal leadership) don't forget to consider your own strengths and how they could be leveraged in a leadership capacity. Leadership doesn't always mean leading large multinational companies. It could also mean establishing an organisation or movement of your own. Leadership doesn't always mean leading from the top or the front. It can also mean leading from within, encouraging others to embrace personal leadership and ownership of their own part in a situation, or simply being an exemplary role model within your community.

Chapter 2

What is the Ambition Revolution?

Chapter 2

What is the Ambition Revolution?

> *"We can start by better defining and modelling ambition for women and girls. We need to ensure that the connotation captures the positives of the concept – making a difference in the world and being one's best self."*
>
> – Mary Wittenberg, global CEO of Virgin Sport

This chapter will help you understand the benefits and possibilities of being ambitious along with the downside of not being ambitious. The ambitious woman stereotype has hugely negative connotations so when we start behaving in ambitious ways it can sometimes lead to feelings of discomfort, be frowned upon by friends and family and openly criticised by others who are challenged or threatened by you. But does it have to be this way? Surely if we work out a way of unpacking some of the characteristics and traits we will learn to understand ourselves more easily and be in a position to confidently and unreservedly tackle ambitious goals and projects.

My goal is to provide you with an alternative roadmap that help you navigate your career more easily. When symptoms or signs of our own mindsets, societal expectations and stereotyped norms arise, it's helpful to have already addressed some of the issues so that you have a choice. We'll look at various stages of ambition, and common characteristics to help you identify the mindsets, misconceptions and momentum required in order to help you navigate your own ambitions more easily.

Growth	Mindset	Impact
Revolutionary	New reality for self & others	10x
Go Getter	Embraces expert status	8x
Achiever	Substantive with a safety line	6x
Schemer	Hand up before you feel ready	4x
Dreamer	Waiting	3x
Operator	Does the job	2x
Observer	Watches passively	-
Detractor	The critic	-

The Ambition Revolution

17

Detractor – the critic

At some stage you may find yourself in Detractor Mode. You'll see on the model that it's at the bottom – and definitely falls into the unambitious category. This is 'the critic' – where we sit on the sidelines with our arms folded across our chest protectively or defensively and only have negative things to say.

"That will never work."

"We tried that five years ago and it was a waste of time."

In terms of getting ahead – tackling big, hairy, audacious goals or ambitions (BHAGs) – it will have negative impact and won't get you very far at all. Find yourself in Detractor Mode for too long and you're definitely on the way out. Change your mind or change your role. The choice is yours.

Observer – passive

You know when you first start in a role and you're really neither in nor out? You haven't committed emotionally, nor do you want to rock the boat until you've had a chance to assess the lay of the land. Or perhaps you find yourself in a situation with a new manager or a new leadership team. You're passively observing before you commit yourself, your energy or your ideas fully. Once again, if you find yourself in Observer Mode you need to move through it swiftly as it won't help in terms of your leadership aspirations to remain passive. Yes, it probably serves a purpose as you evaluate the situation, assess any risk or take stock, but it won't get you ahead very far or very fast. Move out or move up as soon as possible.

Operator – doing the job

We then move over an imaginary line into the Operator phase – otherwise known as 'doing the job'. This is definitely on the positive. It's good to *do the job* as the job needs be done, and there will be times in your career when buckling down and *doing the job* is what's required. However, many of us, including most women, have been socialised into believing that doing the job well is a sure fire way to get ahead. We do the job thoroughly, we do the job well – we polish up doing the job within an inch of its life, imagining it's a fast track to career success. Maybe when you first start out in your career you want a few roles under your belt where you do the job and it pays your way through university, or you do the job well while you build some experience for your resume or in the lower ranks of an organisation. But then you need another string to your bow – doing the job well, plus a range of other tactics. When thinking in terms of ambition, strategically managing your career or tackling big, audacious, projects – doing the job is only one part of a strategy and interestingly at the lower end of the scale. If you have any ambition whatsoever you'll need to do far more than *do the job*.

Dreamer – why women wait

> *"A goal without a plan is just a wish."*
> – Antoine de Saint-Exupery, French writer

This next level is dreamer, and dreaming of something new and different can be really exciting. Don't dream small mind you! After all, it's your dream, so you can be as bold and courageous as you like. Yet, while you see lots of memes on the internet on the power of dreaming – dreaming alone won't get you very far. For many women, the Dreamer Category is characterised by waiting – waiting for someone to notice how well we're doing the job, waiting to be tapped on the shoulder, waiting to feel ready or qualified, waiting to be discovered, waiting for the universe to provide, waiting to be rescued, waiting until the exact right moment, waiting for the kids to have left school, for the partner's risky business ventures to have settled down … the list goes on. Don't get stuck in the rut of dreaming for too long. After all, a dream without action stays as a dream and may turn to regret. A dream without action is hesitation – and hesitation is a known confidence dampener.

Schemer – "Schemers eat Dreamers for breakfast"

In Schemer Mode you:

- Put your hand up before you feel ready

- Embrace *failure practice* and the *rejection game* as worthwhile activities

- See limitations as challenges

- Learn to colour outside the lines

- Fly by the seat of your pants

- Have difficult conversations skilfully

- Tackle risk bravely, and

- Do it all over again as you learn and grow

Schemer Mode is at the cusp of where the magic starts to happen. Once you start Scheming you are well beyond Dreaming. Yet many women even dislike the stereotyped connotations of the label 'Schemer'. However, this is where things start to get concrete and is a critical turning point in your career.

Remember back in primary school, when the teacher would ask a question of the class? The boys in the class would all shoot their hand up to grab the teacher's attention, whether they knew the answer or not. Somehow they knew even then, that it was better to be proactive and have their hand up, rather than wait around to be invited or until they thought they knew the right answer. Perhaps they realised that by the time the teacher got around to asking them, they would have the chance to puzzle it out, or even if they got it wrong, there were no serious consequences. They may have looked a little silly (to the girls) but they actually didn't really care about that either.

Is it possible that the way we socialise young girls to do things right, properly and thoroughly is growing generations of women who are perfectionists, risk averse and keepers of proper behaviour? I don't think that women are the only ones who let perfectionistic tendencies get in the way of good work, but I'm confident that we take that perfectionist label and turn it into a different beast. As adults we are constantly bombarded with images in the media of other women who are thin, glamorous, have great careers, gorgeous husbands and perfectly behaved children, who cook like a *Master Chef* who have houses that could feature in *Vogue Living* magazine and a wardrobe to die for. Even writing this list of things that apparently I should strive for perfection in, I feel destined to fail and guilty about it as well.

Can we have it all? Absolutely, but if and only if, we're prepared to compromise on the notion of perfectionism. Scheming is important, because with scheming comes the notion of volunteering for projects or roles before you feel ready, trying things as a 'suck it and see' approach, simply because you can. We embrace *failure practice* and the *rejection game*, because the more nos you get the closer you are to your yes. We begin to learn that flying by the seat of our pants and being prepared to simply have a crack at it, is sometimes required. We also need to learn to embrace risk as part of getting ahead, not as something to be avoided.

And, because many of these things are going to go against ingrained and socialised tendencies for doing things well, properly, right and appropriately, you may feel very uncomfortable in this mode. Spend too long in Schemer Mode and you'll get worn out and likely drop back down to *waiting* or *doing the job* again. To avoid this, you need resilience strategies. You need support mechanisms to keep you feeling confident, circuit breakers to help keep you from hesitating too long, and a clear understanding that this is normal, not wrong.

The dotted line – "I decide"

Look at the dotted line between Schemer Mode and Achiever Mode. This imaginary line is important because it represents the shift from when your career is something that happens to you, to when you start creating your own career and success. This line represents you accepting responsibility and doing something about it, being accountable – your own authority, agency, self-belief and confidence all rolled into one. This line is so important that I even categorise anything below it as Career Limiting Mindsets (CLM) and anything above it as Career Enhancing Mindsets (CEM). This line represents your willingness to stand up, be counted and take a leadership role – the buck stops with you. My goal as mentor and motivator is to encourage you to dance lightly amongst the three levels above the dotted line.

Achiever – substantive with a safety line

The Achiever Mode truly is where the rubber hits the road. This is the *Step Up* in the book title. You've committed to action, you've taken ownership of your own destiny in terms of career strategy, and you've let go of outdated notions about what it means to succeed or lead. You've managed to land yourself a substantive role or two with an eye to an even more substantive role in the future. The beauty of this phase is that it's likely got a safety net or safety harness of some sort.

You may remember the Hewlett Packard research where they examined internal promotions and the different way that men and women applied for roles. Women tended to only apply for a role if they met five out of the five criteria, whereas men were far more likely to apply for a role even if they only met three out of five of the criteria. My executive recruiter contacts always laugh at this statistic and say that, some men ring them and demand an interview when they only meet one out 10 of the criteria.

At this level you acknowledge it's okay to Step Up into a leadership role, with some support mechanism in place to help you succeed. Ideas for support mechanisms include:

- Not needing to express your own opinion (i.e. the opinion of the Board is the opinion you will be required to express),

- Having your boss as your lifeline, championing and sponsoring you through this next phase of your career,

- Taking on a mentor or two to help you navigate skill sets that are slightly beyond your area of expertise,

- Appointing a high performance coach to help you navigate particularly tricky territory, or

- Employing staff to backfill areas of expertise that aren't your strong suit.

Well done you for making it here! This is a great stage in your career.

Go Getter – embrace your inner expert and start building and enhancing your personal brand

This is the *Speak Out* part of the book title. You've landed your substantive role and you've been in the industry long enough to start embracing expert status. You need to position yourself as a credible expert and gain visibility and recognition both inside and outside of your organisation. You become known for delivering results and for helping others achieve the same results themselves. You are comfortable questioning the status quo and thinking outside the box, because you understand the principles at play.

Did you know that in Australia on the speaker circuit most of the speakers are men? In the consulting world there are far more men than women? I'm going out on a limb here, but I wonder if behind every male CEO who publishes there is a really smart female ghost writer? I'm not saying men make bad speakers or consultants or experts, but that women too can and should aspire to acknowledged expert status. In fact, our corporate and government sectors depend on it. We need to start questioning the status quo and allow for the reality that we women do indeed know what we're talking about. We may or may not have the loudest voice, the fastest decision-making processes or the most competitive approach, but we do know how to work with others, find collaborative solutions, build great teams and communities, drive even better customer satisfaction and manage risk well. We're also great at bridging the gap between operational and strategic – because we've certainly done our time in the more operational areas of the business. Plus if you've been working in a particular area for seven years or more, that's expert status in my book, after all, a PhD takes about seven years to complete. So embrace your new Go Getter Expert Status and head on out and spread the word.

The Revolutionary – creating a new reality for yourself and others

The final stage in The Ambition Revolution ladder is that of The Revolutionary – "If you can't find a seat at the table, bring your own chair". If you don't like the way things are, then change them. And you can't drive the change unless you are prepared to lead. The defining mindset of The Revolutionary is that of creating a new reality for yourself and others.

If you look at various industry categories such as the not-for-profit (NFP) sector, the community sector, the health sector, and education sector – the one thing they have in common is more women in senior leadership roles. Women value making a difference and applying some of the feminine leadership traits that we're socialised around in ways that create change.

Back to you and your situation - have a look at the previous image once more. Where do you sit right now? And where do you want to be?

The Three Pillars of Ambition

The three pillars of ambition are belief, drive and action.

Belief – made up of your beliefs about yourself, your upbringing, what's right or wrong, your work, and the environment you live and operate in. It's complicated and your beliefs are not always logical, rational or helpful, despite us considering ourselves to be rational beings. In fact, if you've done any personal development courses over the years, you will have heard of the term *limiting beliefs*. These are the ideas and notions that we hold to be true yet are totally incongruent with what we are trying to achieve. Belief impacts on a complicated web of confidence, your resilience and your mindset. When your beliefs are congruent, in alignment and pointing in the direction of your choice, you are able to act with a degree of fearlessness, courage and confidence, which in turn will boost your ability to get ahead.

While the positive psychology movement is criticised at times for being too simplified ("you need to believe and you will succeed"), you can't deny the role of positive self-belief in success. But if your beliefs are not aligned, you'll struggle, which will feed any negative beliefs, cause low confidence and make it less likely you will want to get of your comfort zone in the future.

Three Pillars of Ambition

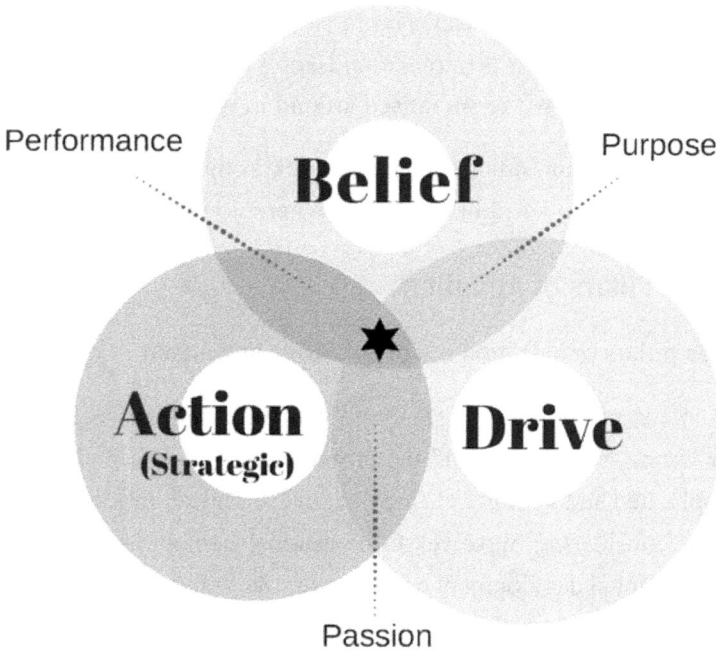

Performance   **Belief**   Purpose

Action
(Strategic)   **Drive**

Passion

The Ambition Revolution
© 2016 amandablesing.com all rights reserved

Drive – the driving force behind your desire to get ahead, to do good work, to make a difference. Unique to everyone and made up of things that are important to you, your values, your upbringing, societal expectations, your fears about not succeeding. If you tease out drive you'll see it impacts on your aspirations, determination and your motivation. Think about the following list of things that are important to you and other people about work:

- Salary

- Opportunity to make a difference and contribute

- Respect of peers and colleagues

- Autonomy

- Lifestyle

- Opportunity to prove yourself

- Progress

- Learning

- Intellectual challenge

And the list continues . . and is unique to you at this point of time.

Possible conflicts between belief and drive

You may find that one or two of your priorities are incongruent with a belief you hold.

- Example 1: Belief – *Rich people are fat cats and lazy.* If one of your priorities is to make a kick-ass salary, you can imagine that this belief is going to get in the way of your big salary drivers and undermine your salary goals or your willingness and ability to negotiate.

- Example 2: Belief – *You have to work hard to get ahead.* If you are aiming for fast track career success, yet one of your priorities is work–life balance, then this work hard belief and your work–life balance priority are going to clash at some stage. Without knowing it, you leave yourself open to self-sabotage – at every critical moment, every last minute deadline or every major project that requires significant effort.

- Example 3: Belief – *Work should be easy, something I'm naturally gifted and talented at so that it doesn't take up much effort.* If one of your priorities is learning or intellectually challenging work, and yet you keep applying for roles that are easy and you could do with one hand tied behind your back, then not only will you find yourself easily bored, but you won't be stretching yourself to your maximum capacity – under utilising your talents and undermining your own career every step of the way.

You can see how this works and how easy it is for things to get confused without you being aware. Take time out at the end of this chapter to tackle the optional exercises and do your own work before continuing on.

Action – there are two components of action to explore.

Acton part 1 – The action that comes from making a decision and then committing to action. You decide, then you act. You can think about washing the dishes, you can look at the pile of dirty dishes and wish they were washed, but until you take action to wash those dishes (or even to ask someone to wash the dishes) they remain unwashed. You saw in the Dreamer Category that we women wait. We wait for the time to be right, to feel ready, for circumstances to feel more certain before making a decision to act, for it to be more convenient. At some stage this waiting gets in the way of taking action – simply making a decision and giving it a crack. Hesitation causes mayhem to momentum, and is a confidence-killer all in one. Action precedes clarity and confidence. Take action now.

From my own experience, for many years I explored the option of breaking into the real estate market here in Melbourne and purchasing a unit. If you are from Australia, you will know that Melbourne has some of the most expensive real estate in the world. I thought about it a lot. I researched buying a unit. I could quote prices of units in my suburb and the surrounding suburbs. I'd even consulted several mortgage brokers multiple times to help me arrange pre-approval for finance. Yet I still hesitated. I waited. By the time I finally purchased a unit, I had waited for nearly ten years. In those ten years prices of units in my desired area had increased dramatically, that I estimate I paid $300K more than if I had bought when I first started investigating. I also wasted a lot of time and energy with reworking figures and numbers, inspecting properties and meeting with mortgage broker after mortgage broker. Guess who wishes she committed to action ten years prior? However, it's what we do with learnings like this that count. I can do nothing, or use this as a salutary (and expensive) lesson on the benefits of taking action more rapidly.

In his book *Think, Decide, Act*, author and emergency management expert Russell Boon shares how good decision-making, even in critical moments, sometimes comes best from intuition, inner wisdom and experience – rather than spreadsheets and over-preparing. His favourite mantra? *Any decision, even the wrong decision is better than no decision.* Why? Because if you don't have enough evidence about a possible decision, then you simply make any decision, and more evidence will come to light enabling you to either commit to the decision or course correct and continue. Whereas if you hesitated, you'd still be sitting there with no more evidence, and no further along towards your goal.

Action part 2 (Strategic Action) – Most women are busy 'doing the do'. As you saw in Operator Category, we're socialised to 'do the job', do good work, to do the right thing, to get things done, and at times we wear ourselves out with this action component. You've probably heard the expression 'give a busy woman something to do' with the unsaid portion of the statement being 'she'll get it done'. How many times have you heard a woman at work say 'oh give it to me, I'll do it, it will be easier'? Sheryl Sandberg and Adam Grant in their New York Times article *Madam CEO Get Me a Coffee* wrote about women doing the office housework, taking care of others, making sure things are done properly and all the pieces are picked up. Not only is the office housework a choice, but it's also expected of women. However, these behaviours aren't getting us ahead. In fact, they seem to get in the way. When you stop and think about it, organisations run better with people who behave that way, and don't ask for more money for doing so – it's in the short term interests of the organisation to keep those who do office housework doing the office housework. But it doesn't translate into career success, more substantive or meaty projects, or more money – for women – or those benefits of increased performance for organisations. The irony being that when men do help out with these office chores they are complimented, commended and get to bask in the resulting glory.

Stop Being Busy and Start Being Strategic

Many of my female clients are high achievers, who pride themselves on being super-efficient, able to get huge volumes of work done both at home and at the office. In all likelihood they've had to be in order to survive and to get to where they have already in terms of work and career. This is not a criticism and let me be clear – it takes one to know one. But is doing everything, being superhuman and getting huge volumes of work done sustainable or strategic?

Being strategic is the qualifier. Efficiency is one thing, but effectiveness is definitely better. If your goal is to lead, then prioritise being strategic about the most effective steps to creating leadership opportunities. If your goal is to launch a successful global brand then prioritise the strategy required to achieve that successful launch. Within the requirement to take action, strategic action is even better.

But in saying that, don't let perfect be the enemy of good. Any action is better than no action. Get moving now.

Many people talk about the 80:20 rule – the Pareto Principle. When we're looking at our career and possible progression, hopefully in an upwardly mobile trajectory, we are frequently running blind. No-one really knows the play book. No-one really knows what works and, with so many variables at play. who could? The question remains, if we're supposed to be focusing on the 20% of the work that will contribute 80% of the result, how do we really know which 20% that is? We don't.

The first step under Strategic Action is to eliminate things that we know that will get in the way of getting ahead. And the second step is to then start leveraging your inner wisdom, experience and network to tap into what really does work and simply focus on that.

The Intersections Between the Three Pillars

Passion – How do you find your passion? Ask yourself:

- What lights you up?
- What makes you get out of bed every day and go do great work?
- What would you be prepared to do for free?
- If money were no barrier, what would you do?

One of my clients works in a highly conservative role in a large organisation. She is great at her role and right now learning to position herself as an expert so she can more easily leverage her newly defined personal brand in the future. When I asked her what she'd do if money were no object she answered "I'd like to learn to fly a helicopter". I'd hazard a guess that in the future the next organisation she chooses to work for will be less conservative than the one she is currently with.

Purpose – What's your *why*?

> *"People don't buy what you do, they buy why you do it."* – Simon Sinek

When leading the peak body for those in the consumer affairs industry one of the thing that I admired most about the members was their clearly defined *why*. Let's face it – complaints management is not the sexiest topic or easiest job around. But these people were passionate about it. And the thing I liked most was that they could clearly articulate their *why* – "providing access to justice for consumers". If truth be told, this clearly defined purpose was so appealing to me that I wanted to feel the same way about something.

Harvard Psychologist Amy Cuddy in her book *Presence: Bringing Your Boldest Self to Your Biggest Challenges* talks about the importance of being able to unpack your why and how a deep connection to your sense of purpose improves your performance. She calls this presence – the natural passion, enthusiasm and authenticity that shines through as a result.

Taylor Clark, journalist and author of *Nerve: Poise Under Pressure, Serenity Under Stress, and the Brave New Science of Fear and Cool*, unpacks some of the science behind fear and stress, and how being closely connected to your why helps you perform far better in stressful situations - performing seemingly impossible feats with relative grace and ease.

When connected to their why;

- Fire-fighters or trauma surgeons are able to perform the dangerous, amazing and impossible far more easily

- Entrepreneurs pitching for funding have greater success,

- Interview candidates come across far more confidently, capably and authentically, and

- Speakers on stage are able to deliver far more powerful and memorable messages and perform better.

And why? This *why* connection somehow short circuits the production of stress hormones and enables you to perform at your best without the Amygdala Hijack getting in the way (flight, fight or freeze sympathetic nervous body response).

For example, I'm really nervous about public speaking. In fact, six years ago when my own coach suggested that as part of my thought leadership journey I'd need to speak in public, I closed the conversation down. Immediately. I wanted no part of the public speaking journey because it scared me senseless - literally. While I'd booked and briefed more speakers than most people have had hot dinners, I couldn't see myself naturally succeeding. I'd had a few experiences where I'd been forced to speak in public and the memories weren't great regarding the results. Not only was my performance fairly average, but the remembered stress was overwhelming.

However, when I finally found my *why*, around helping women in (and into) leadership roles, it became obvious, that if I were to make any serious impact and help more women, then I'd need to learn to manage my fear of public speaking. I could help a limited number of women one on one ... or I could speak to many and inspire far more in larger groups.

My *why* helps me navigate my nerves far more easily on stage. My *why* keeps me focused even when I feel ill before heading on stage. My *why* keeps me keeping on even when I don't perform at my best, because it's never about me, but always about the difference I can make in someone else's life.

What about you? What's your why? Consider the following:

- Is it to provide opportunities for your children?

- Is it that you want to help people in some way?

- Is it that you want to create change in a situation – business, financial, political, environmental, human rights?

- What makes you go do things that you are uncomfortable with, because you know you can do more good in this uncomfortable situation, than sitting safely behind a desk?

Start reflecting and journaling. Talk with friends.

Once you connect to your *why*, you may be surprised about what courageous work is possible for you to tackle.

And finally, **Performance**, and here is where we see some alchemy.

As you've already read, belief is made up in part of beliefs about yourself, which contribute to your feelings of confidence – or lack thereof. When we have low confidence we are far more likely to hesitate. Yet hesitation in and of itself contributes to lower confidence – a classic Catch-22.

The fix for low confidence is action. Remember - action precedes clarity and confidence. The fix for hesitation is increased confidence. Get started and take action and your performance increases, whether you are focused on it or not.

Optional Exercises

Exercise 1: What to you believe about ...

Ask yourself the following questions and jot down the first four or five things that come to mind. Don't think about it too much. Once you've identified what it is you believe about these key issues, examine them for any incongruence, then journal and explore how you came to these beliefs, where these beliefs and notions came from and are they helpful or not helpful.

- What do you believe about work?

- What do you believe about ambition?

- What do you believe about success?

- What do you believe about great leadership?

- What do you believe about money?

- What do you believe about women and work?

For example: if you believe that great leaders are strong, powerful and tall, and you are a short, diminutive and not as strong – you are undermining yourself and your leadership goals from the get go. You could address the external issues (i.e. wear heels, give strong commands in a deep voice) or you could do the internal work and examine where these ideas of successful leaders came from, and uncover the source of your discomfort.

Ask yourself:

- Where did these ideas come from?

- Is there any evidence that these ideas aren't always true? Are there role models of great leaders who aren't tall, strong and powerful?

- In fact, is there any evidence in which being powerful, strong and tall gets in the way of great leadership?

- Is this belief a help or a hindrance?

Then decide to keep the belief, or let it go.

> Note: re not thinking about things too much - the more flippant your statements the more likely they are to have come from that part of your brain that doesn't analyse, the deep ingrained machinery of your mind, your automatic thinking. This is the material that will give you most reward.

Exercise 2: What's important to you about work?

Grab a pen and paper and list all the things that are important to you about work. You want to fill an A4 page at the very least.

When the easy answers run out, try asking yourself the question in another way – "What might be important to someone else about work? "

Once again, freely jot down your answers. Don't analyse, rationalise or categorise. Write them down.

Once you have run out of answers and your page is full, then take a moment to reflect. If you could only choose eight items on this list, what would they be? This time, do put numbers next to your list (1–8) but don't prioritise yet. The numbers are simply to help you to easily keep count.

The final step is to reread your top eight items on the list with a non-critical mind, and reflect. Then ask yourself: "If I found myself in a situation where I could only have three items on my list, what would my top three be?" This is the time to categorise, to sort and prioritise.

Sometimes these priorities will be obvious and clear cut and sometimes they won't be. Remember, the priorities you have selected are right for now, in this moment. They may change in time.

Exercise 3: Drain and sustain audit

Grab your journal. Draw a line down the middle of page and on the left hand side list the things that drain you and on the right hand side the things that sustain you. By drain, I mean the things that wear you out –your obligations, activities with emotional baggage attached, or activities that you may simply have outgrown. For example, a few years ago I created a group on Facebook in the yoga teacher community here in Melbourne that truly flourished. I'm a yoga teacher plus I have a 20 year career history in servicing professions. I saw a gap and I created a group to help fill that gap. I then became the administrator of the group. However, as the group grew and the administrative burden became heavier, and my interest in the 'administrivia' diminished, I became increasingly drained by the activity. After months of angst and denial, I finally pinpointed this activity as something that drained me and found another solution that was better suited for the group. I still maintain some connection to the group because I believe in the values and the help that the active group provides but for a range of reasons the administrative work no longer nourished me.

Consider things in your work and life that exhaust or drain you, such as:

- Housework

- Ironing

- Reconciling your credit card

- Invoicing

- Scheduling/confirming meetings

- Committee administration

- Meetings with no agendas or clear outcomes

- Cleaning up the office kitchen

- Unofficial mentoring/mothering of others at work

- Commute time

- Following up on unpaid invoices

- Taking calls from staff, clients or customers about FAQs

- Feeling guilty about not exercising or not spending enough time with the kids

Once you've identified what drains you, work out how to either eliminate those things, do them differently, make them less of a 'chore', delegate them entirely or work out how to make them more sustaining.

Note: this drain or sustain exercise is not limited to either work or home. For example, one of the things we women have going against us when it comes to career success is our wardrobe, fashion and deciding what to wear in the morning. Men in general wear suits. Women have myriad items to choose from including suits.

We've all read about people like US President Barack Obama and Apple's Steve Jobs having a really limited wardrobe to help eliminate fashion faux pas at work. Great idea. Another benefit of this approach is that it keeps your decision-making muscle and abilities fresh You aren't wearing out your decision making abilities on things that (on a scale of trivial to life threatening/sustaining) aren't that important.

After all, most of us are super-efficient when we travel for business because we usually only take one or two outfits away with us – certainly minimising choice. This means we are able to get up, get going and tackle big issues without the distraction of wardrobe choices or the risk of potential fashion faux pas.

If you are one of those people who spend considerable time in the morning trying on different tops, pants or skirts in an effort to find the right outfit to wear, why not change this? On the weekend set aside some time to reflect and make a plan for what you'll wear for the entire week. Don't forget shoes and accessories. Be strategic.

Consider taking this to the next level by working with a stylist to truly help you create an easy range of wardrobe choices that are efficient AND effective.

And stylists aren't only for women. My father is a classic example of a male who, with the help of a stylist, has been able to extend the effectiveness and length of his career in the agricultural sector long beyond the age when most consultants retire. As a farmer, my father's choice in work attire had definite room for improvement once he relocated to the city. He was carving out a new career for himself in the boardroom and as a consultant prior to retirement and identified his need for a more effective wardrobe as something he could do with expert assistance in. With the guidance of a stylist his new suits take 15 years off of his appearance. The family laugh about it and love it at the same time. Who ever heard of a farmer hiring a stylist? Not us! But as incongruous as it is, it works for him and ...... it may also work for you.

However, not only does his new stylish wardrobe means he looks a million bucks, but there is far less room for error and he feels more confident - with confidence once again being key. When we feel confident we are far more likely to get out of our comfort zone, stretch for opportunities beyond our immediate reach or volunteer for projects that we've never tackled before.

To cut a long story short – work out what drains you and what sustains you, what supports you and what undermines you. Then identify how to move the activities that drain you into a more sustainable form, or eliminate them altogether – leaving you more time to do the work you love doing, be with the people you love hanging out with and making a difference in your work, career and life far more easily.

Chapter 3

What's in it for You?

Chapter 3

What's in it for You?

"Men look in the mirror and see a senator, and women look in and see somebody who needs more experience." – Anne E Korblut

So far we've learned all about why feminine ambition is good for business – profitability, productivity, risk, customer satisfaction and staff engagement to name a few. We've even examined why feminine ambition is good for society – men and women included – including social innovation, different thinking, inclusiveness, solving old problems in new ways. But we haven't yet really explored why it's good for you personally. This section is all about the 'What's in it for me' factor. Why should you bother?

The Feminine Ambition Trifecta

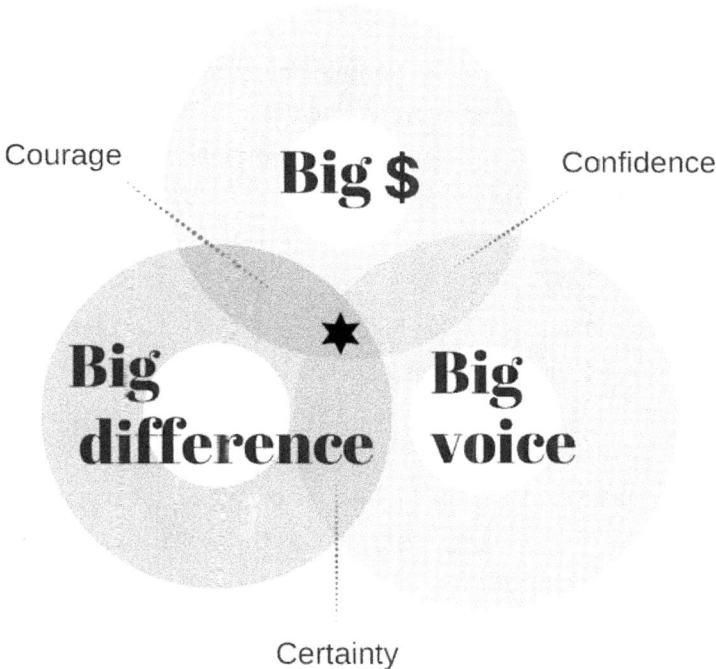

The Feminine Ambition Trifecta

Courage

Big $

Confidence

Big difference

★

Big voice

Certainty

The Ambition Revolution

There is a myth out there that women are less ambitious than men. I challenge this assumption. What we know from research into gender differences and ambition is that it's far more likely that we simply measure and value ambition differently. Men tend to measure their ambition and success by way of financial gain. They land a promotion with a big pay rise and are seen as ambitious and successful. We socialise our boys to think and behave this way. It's even expected of them. On the other hand, the literature tells us that women, in addition to aspiring to earn more money, *also* want to know that we're *being heard* and *making a difference.*[1][2] And if we don't feel like we're being heard, or we don't feel like we're making a difference, we're far more likely to *lean out*, find something else, make a sideways move, take another role where we feel as though our voice is being heard, that we're contributing in meaningful ways – despite the money.

My goal is to help you win the feminine ambition trifecta – earn a great salary, develop a voice that is heard, and make an even bigger difference. Because organisations, governments and communities need more women – plus it will be good for you as well.

Remuneration

Salary is one of the reasons that both men and women are ambitious. Your socialisation and values probably dictate whether your salary goals are purely about paying the bills and saving for a rainy day, or measuring your sense of achievement via financial gain. One of the expectations about being ambitious is that the higher up the food chain you go, the bigger the salary. But is this the case? Amongst Australia's ASX listed CEOs, the women aren't paid as much as their peers, yet are performing in some instances much better. However recent research also indicates that when an industry becomes more feminised the average salary decreases as reported in the New York Times in early 2016. According to Sociology Professor Paula England from New York University, once women start doing a job it doesn't look like it's as important to the bottom line, or require as much skill.

This is gender bias, pure and simple.

---

1   *"Compared to Men, Women View Professional Advancement as Equally Attainable, but Less Desirable."* Proceedings of the National Academy of Sciences of the United States of America (in press). Gino, Francesca, Caroline Ashley Wilmuth, and Alison Wood Brooks

2   Integrating work and life: It's not just a woman's issue anymore. Julie Coffman, Priscilla Schenck and Melissa Artabane, Bain & Company

Gender salary gap

We've already identified that money is only one of the drivers for feminine endeavour with making a difference and being heard also being important. However, the ramifications for women not having money as a key driver are significant.

In 1969 in Australia there was a legally mandated salary gap of 25% in many industries. Yes, you read that correctly. Given that Australia was one of the leaders in giving women the vote, I find this surprising.

Spring forward to 2016 and there remains a totally non-mandated salary gap of 16.2% (2016 WGEA results), and it steadily fluctuates year upon year between 16% and 19%.

In almost 50 years we've moved the gender salary gap by 9% and this improvement ranges between 6% and 9% year on year. Not particularly inspiring is it? We've worked 'hard' at this for years. I say it's now time to work far smarter.

Some other interesting facts to make your eyes water;

- Overall, women make up 46.2% of the Australian workforce, but currently earn 16.2 % less than men.

- The higher a woman rises through the ranks, the larger the pay gap is going to be with recent research indicating that this gap equates to approximately $100K per year for top tier managers. See:

  https://www.wgea.gov.au/media-releases/report-shows-100k-gender-pay-gap-top-tier-managers

- In 2015, ANZ quantified the gender salary gap as adding up to $700K over the course of a career, but more recent research now sheds more light on this and says that over the course of a lifetime a woman can expect to earn $1.5million less than a man – and it even starts at home with differences in pocket money. See:

http://www.abc.net.au/news/2016-03-07/gender-pay-gap-starts-in-childhood-actu/7225924

One of the biggest wake-up calls for me was watching an episode of Australian comedian Judith Lucy's television show *Is All Woman*, where she tackled the topic of ageing. She bemoans with a group of other women about their retirement funds (or lack thereof).

Did you know that:

- 60% of women aged 65–69 have no superannuation at all?
- And almost 40% of single women will retire into poverty?

If we go right back to when men and women first enter the workforce as graduates, we begin to see a very interesting picture. Professor Linda Babcock of Carnegie Mellon University and the author of *Women Don't Ask* has found that *"Men initiate salary negotiations four times as often as women do, and that when women do negotiate, on average they ask for 30% less money than men do."*

Marilyn Davidson from the Manchester Business School in the UK asks her students each year what they expect to earn, and what they deserve to earn, five years after graduation. *"On average the men think they deserve $80,000 a year and the women $64,000 – or 20% less."*

My recruiter contacts here in Australia share with me that even at the initial interview with a recruiter they see most women candidates asking for at least $20K less than men per annum.

What with women starting on a lower salary, then not asking for increases, and if they do ask, wear the risk of being considered greedy, taking career breaks for family or study, not negotiating as hard when they have the opportunity, not being offered or considered for the same higher salaried opportunities, combined with biases both conscious and unconscious – we will need to stay in the workforce for longer before we can retire unless we do something about it now. Once again, according to ANZ's report, we'll need to stay in workforce about 15 years longer in order to retire on the same level of superannuation.

What are some of the contributing factors behind these discrepancies?

- Discrimination – where women aren't even considered for leadership or higher salaried opportunities because they appear to lack 'vertical ambition' as we recently saw in the Saatchi & Saatchi incident in 2016. More generally because women don't necessarily demonstrate ambition in the same ways as men do, they are excluded.

- Unconscious bias – where men and women judge a woman negatively if she negotiates too hard, or if she sings her own praises, amongst other things

- Lack of confidence when it comes to asking for a raise – there are multiple studies now proving that when it comes to negotiation on their own behalf in general women are less confident than men

- Socialisation – young girls socialised to not rock the boat, with the concept of the ideal woman being that she is diminutive, likeable and reliant on others to take care of her, probably having considerable impact

- Lack of societal expectation for women to be the breadwinner or take the lead with salary (although we are seeing more and more role reversal in recent years).

- Roles that are deemed to be 'women's work' and are paid less well i.e. secretarial, administration support and child care

- Career breaks and flexible arrangements to raise children or undertake further study

Then if we move into accepting some responsibility for the part that we as women play in perpetuating this cycle:

- Not asking – whether we don't want to rock the boat or we don't understand we're supposed to ask, we simply don't ask as frequently (or for as much) as men

- Not understanding the rules of the career advancement game

- When asked in a performance appraisal about how we went, we modestly describe the process and where things went wrong, instead of talking up the achievements

- We wait to be noticed for doing good work, instead of going out and telling others about the strategic benefit we're adding to the business.

If any of the above resonated for you then the chapter on negotiation tactics for women is a must read. Additionally, individuals need to tackle this strategically and organisations need to put circuit breakers in place. My personal belief is that until there is a sting in the tail, such as bonuses not paid for non-compliance, or Boards, governments and shareholders enforcing the issue, then the gender pay gap will continue to be glacially slow to close.

Having a Say and Being Heard

We understand notionally that when women are on the leadership team equally with men, organisations frequently perform better on a range of measures. But there is more to being on the leadership team than being on the team for the sake of meeting targets or ratios – although this does help. We also need to feel as though our contribution is valued. We want to have a say, for our opinions to carry equal weight as those of our male peers and colleagues, we want our arguments to be heard and for both men and women to value them.

One of the struggles of the gender diversity and inclusion movement is that sometimes women are appointed onto the leadership team their opinions are excluded. As the analogy goes – we are invited to the party, but no-one wants to dance with us.

There are a bunch of made up terms that I enjoy which illustrate some of the things that can go wrong:

- *Bropropriation* – when a woman suggests something it's overlooked but when a male suggests the same thing everyone thinks it's a great idea

- *Manterruptions* – where men speak over women which discounts the woman's argument. You see this in social interactions as well, when you ask a woman a question and her male partner answers for her

- *Mansplaining* – where a man will explain to 'the little woman' something she already knows about or is expert in.

This is an amusing use of language to describe the problem and even pigeonholing all men into one category as well.

Having a say, feeling like your opinion is valued, equally weighted, valid and important goes a long way towards making the shift from:

- Feeling defensive to feeling self-assured,

- Feeling like you need to prove our worth, to simply feeling worthy and

- Feeling like you need to convince others to our way of thinking, to having solid conviction in your beliefs, opinions and place in the leadership team.

When women don't have a say, despite having a seat at the table, once again, we are far more likely to want to *lean out,* to not want to contribute any more, to go elsewhere.

Making a Difference

> *"Success isn't about how much money you make, it's about the difference you make in people's lives."* – Michelle Obama

One of the benefits of you leading is that the more opportunities you take in *Stepping Up, Speaking Out and Taking Charge*, the more responsibility will be available to you, and the more opportunity you will have to make a bigger difference. Feminine leadership attributes such as collaboration, inclusive decision-making and emotional intelligence are the new black when it comes to solving 21st century problems – business or social. However if making a difference is so important to us, why do we hesitate?

2011 Institute of Leadership and Management Research report *Ambition and Gender at Work* found that half of the female managers surveyed expressed self-doubt, compared to less than 30% of the men.

Additionally, women are far more likely to underrate their future performance in a non-stereotypical pursuit than men – for example, in a science test. In 2003 Cornell researchers, Dunning and Ehrlinger, ran an experiment to see if women's preconceived notions of their ability would impact on their confidence, and yes they did. Men and women were asked how well they thought they'd perform on a science test. The men tended to overestimate their result and the women underestimated theirs.

Where this gets really interesting is the flow-on effect and real world impact of underestimation. After the test, in which both men and women achieved almost identical results, they were then invited to participate in a science competition. At this stage the students still didn't know how they had actually performed in the test. Only 49% of women decided to participate in the science competition, compared with 71% of the men.

> *"That was a proxy for whether women might seek out certain opportunities ... Because they are less confident in general in their abilities, that led them not to want to pursue future opportunities."*
>
> – Joyce Ehrlinger

Further, in a 2016 study at the University of Michigan, researchers found that women tend to shy away from opportunities where there is more competition. See:

http://psychcentral.com/news/2016/05/15/womens-preference-for-smaller-competition-may-help-explain-pay-gap/103282.html

> *"When applying for a job or college, women seek positions with fewer applicants than men."* – Kathrin Hanek, PhD

Apparently women, more so than men who are stereotypically more competitive, prefer smaller groups to compete in and this consistent gender difference can be applied in a range of contexts.

Isn't it highly likely that the opportunities for making a bigger difference are highly sought after by both men and women? C-suite leadership, Board leadership, ownership of businesses and entrepreneurial ventures are all likely to require a high degree of competition.

In December 2015, *The Australian* published a list of CEOs, including value delivered to shareholders compared to salary. Out of 300 names, 15 were women, of which three were in the top ten in terms of delivering shareholder value. This is a great example of women making a significant difference – to the bottom line of their organisations. Critically, these women are role models for others wanting to make a substantive difference to their organisations and industries despite highly competitive environments. (As an aside these women were nearly all receiving a salary well below their male peers.)

If you are indeed driven by a need to make a bigger difference then finding ways to bolster your confidence in the face of competition would be highly recommended – because those opportunities will be highly competitive for both men and women and you can make a far bigger difference when you are leading.

Why is this important for you personally?

So, let's extrapolate. When you are uncertain or less confident about your abilities to *Step Up, Speak Out and Take Charge* (remember stereotypically, leadership is still seen as the domain of men), you are less likely to even want to participate in leadership. When you regularly underestimate our own potential performance you won't try as hard or stretch as far. When you prefer less competitive environments you are far more likely to avoid situations where a highly competitive nature is required – and ambition and leadership requires competition.

Over my career, I've learned to not trust my own judgment if I suspect there is a hint of underestimation going on. I remember one particular role that I saw advertised and hesitated over applying for. Something prompted me to check in with a friend in another industry – who couldn't believe I even needed to ask as she thought the role was me down to a tee. As per her encouragement, I applied, won the role and was subsequently told that my application including my expertise and experience were such a stand out than I was the only obvious choice. However, that wasn't how I interpreted the situation at the time.

When we have more certainty about our ability to tackle ambitious goals or projects, we are far more likely to give it a go.

Stretch

I call this ability to get out of your own way, to tackle BHAGs with some level of confidence, courage and certainty, 'stretch'. Stretch occurs when you get out of your comfort zone and achieve something you didn't even know was possible. When stretch goals and rewards align, you can find the sweet spot – your calling.

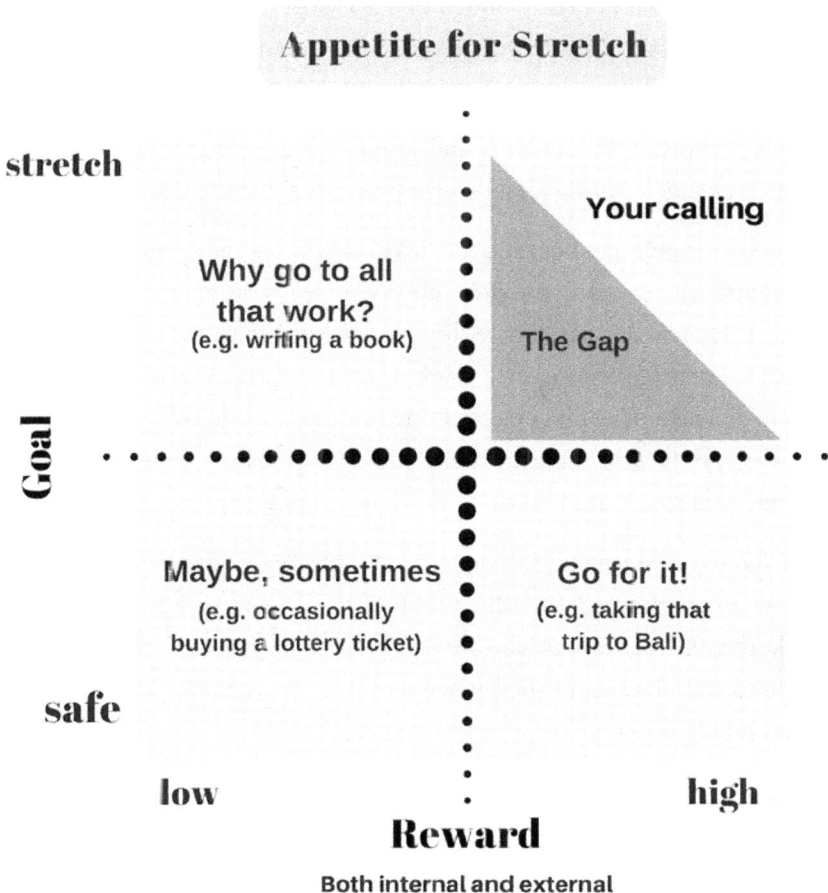

Appetite for Stretch

stretch

Your calling

Why go to all
that work?
(e.g. writing a book)

The Gap

Goal

Maybe, sometimes
(e.g. occasionally
buying a lottery ticket)

Go for it!
(e.g. taking that
trip to Bali)

safe

low   high

Reward

Both internal and external

The Ambition Revolution

The benefits of stretching can be considerable. Let's have a look at the model on the previous page.

- On the left hand side, we have the Stretch axis – with low stretch and high stretch at either end of the range.

- On the bottom axis we have Reward ranging from low to high.

- In the bottom left corner, we have something with a safe goal (easily achievable) but not really much in it for you – there's not much skin in the game either way for you if you do or do not tackle it.

- In the bottom right corner, we have that goal that is high on Rewards but safe in terms of Stretch. Pure and simple this is pleasure – it won't drive much change or bring about world peace, but is certainly nice to have.

- On the top left hand corner, we have something that is high in Stretch and low in Reward. As right now you are reading my first book I can categorically say that writing a book fits into this category. The writing and publishing of a book is going to give me some reward – kudos, sense of achievement, knowing that I'm helping people – but it's certainly not going to make me rich or land me heaps of work compared to the amount of work I need to put in.

- In the top right hand corner, we have the high Stretch and the high Reward quadrant. This is the realm of thrill seekers, adventurers, risk takers and leaders the world over. Where the risks are there causing you to stretch even further, when and if you do achieve your goal will feel much sweeter.

In a regular quadrant model, the aim is to change your behaviours and mindset so you can move towards performing in alignment with the top right hand quadrant, but with this model there is something that gets in the way. This is what I call the *Perception Gap* and it's amplified by the *Stereotype Threat*.

- *Perception Gap* – the difference between your estimaticn of what you will be able to achieve, and what you are actually capable of.

- *Stereotype Threat* – where you feel threatened or challenged when you are required to behave in a way that's non-stereotypical. For the purpose of this argument, when women are asked to do something that they are not stereotypically good at, they are more likely to underestimate their performance but then also less likely to stretch.

This gap in perception about your abilities to stretch, especially when it comes to activities that are stereotypically non-feminine, is where women need to focus. When we have more women leaders as role models, with feminine achievement and ambition being documented as part of our social histories, and there are increased opportunities for women to stretch and be acknowledged for that stretch, this gap will shrink and women will be as likely as men to put their hand up for stretch opportunities.

Remember, my goal for you is the feminine ambition trifecta – I want you to be paid well, to feel like you are being heard/have a voice and to know you are making an even bigger difference.

Chapter 4

Challenging Beliefs and Assumptions

Chapter 4

Challenging Beliefs and Assumptions

It's okay to have big goals and ambitions. And while many men and women still (strangely) believe that having ambition is an unappealing quality in a woman, ambition in and of itself is *not* a dirty word. It's okay to go for what you want or even stretch for something you don't even know exists yet!

In order to lead effectively there are a range of things you may need to let go of. In fact, embracing and embodying confidence around your ability to Step Up, Speak Out and Take Charge ironically requires letting go of sometimes counterintuitive mindsets and behaviours including:

- The need to do it all (Operator)

- The need for approval or to be liked (Dreamer)

- The need to do things perfectly (Schemer)

- The need to know everything (Achiever)

- The need to be right (Go Getter)

- The need to be in control (Revolutionary)

Letting go of the need to do it all – so that you have capacity to think and or behave another way.

As you now know, the Operator gains satisfaction and reward from doing the job – doing it well, doing it rigorously and properly. When someone asks "Can I help?" the Operator is more likely to have internal mental scripts running that say "No, leave it with me because at least I'll know it's being done properly". The Operator also derives value out of working hard and doing it all. Next time you hear yourself say "Give it to me, at least I know it will be done quickly and properly", put the brakes on and ask yourself if that's the only answer. Hard work and doing it all are strategies that keep you worn out, less likely to see new alternatives and stuck in a rut, which you can read more about later in this chapter..

In order to leave Operator Mode, you are going to need to leave behind your need to do it all. Your sense of identity may be challenged but you're going to have to learn to cut corners, delegate, or hand over the reins to someone else. Plus it will help them in their own *Step Up, Speak Out, Take Charge* journey.

Letting go of the need for approval from others – so that you don't
care as much about how others think of you.

> *"The question isn't who is going to let me: it's who is going to stop me."*
>
> – Ayn Rand

As a Dreamer you are likely to have put your own dreams on hold and have probably;

- Put other people's needs before your own

- Given other people's opinion and authority more importance or credibility than your own

- Been worried about whether other people like you or not.

When you can let go of what other people think you are far more likely to commit to action. And remember, the science of confidence teaches us that action is critical in terms of both boosting confidence and moving in the direction of your choice.

As a kid growing up, I remember hearing a constant refrain of "what will the neighbours think?" I can laugh about it now, but you can imagine how that phrase, and what it represented, became part of my blueprint. In hindsight it would have been more helpful for me to learn to call upon what I thought, my own values, my own ethics, my own drivers and goals. But then hindsight is always 20:20 vision.

- Are you putting other people's needs before your own?

- Are you waiting for a tap on the shoulder, or some sign of approval from others?

- Do you need to check your opinion against someone else before expressing it?

- Do you find that you defer to authority figures even if they're not always right?

Learning to question, challenge, act without the endorsement of others or the safety net of likeability can be liberating. Letting go of the need for approval is part and parcel of this.

Letting go of the need to be perfect

Perfectionism is a big issue for women. Many would consider themselves less feminine when not striving for perfectionism in some aspect of their life. Aiming for average is simply not an option. But when we let go of the need to do things perfectly then there is far more room in your life to experiment, embrace new ideas and quite possibly have it all.

My mother tells a story from her school days. As a young woman there were times when she was a model student, doing things right, properly, appropriately and well. In fact, she was so good at doing things well, that the teacher used to seat her next to the less well behaved male students in order to model good behaviour to them. (I hear this is a tactic still used by some teachers today).

She laughingly recounts that there was one particular boy who she was seated next to because he used to do his art and craft *all wrong* – for example he would paint trees the wrong colours. Years later my mother reflects that perhaps he had the right of it because while she has had a long and meaningful career as a teacher, he has gone on to win international acclaim as a successful artist.

It's hard to *fly by the seat of your pants* when everything has to be done 'just so'. It's even more difficult to *colour outside the lines* when you need to colour in exactly right.

Letting go of the need to know everything

> *"Don't be intimidated by what you don't know. That can be your greatest strength and ensure that you do things differently from everyone else."* – Sarah Blakely, Spanx

It's okay to take the promotion, without knowing everything before you land the role. It's a given that for some of the items on the list of criteria on the position description you'll have experience and expertise in, and for others, you'll need a safety net. Your ability to learn on the fly, surround yourself with technical experts and adapt to uncertainty are assets in your career tool belt that will stand you in good stead. Additionally by bringing a new perspective to a role, you will bring new ideas and innovation, along with the creativity to solve old problems in new ways.

Letting go of the need to be right – so that you can embrace your inner expert more easily

> *"The need to be right all the time is the biggest bar to new ideas. It is better to have enough ideas for some of them to be wrong than to be always right by having no ideas at all."* – Edward de Bono

I've never felt confident in terms of debate and logical argument, particularly not when put on the spot or if I am feeling under pressure. I spent six years working with lawyers who are trained and skilful in verbal argument. This cemented my belief that I'd never be as good as some.

However, as my goal is to inspire women to *Step Up, Speak Out and Take Charge* – there are going to be times when I can have the biggest impact on stage or in speaking to groups which requires me not only speaking out, but feeling like I'm under pressure as well.

The 'old' me would have simply assumed that this type of argument was not accessible for me. However, by letting go of the need to be right, then all of a sudden voicing an opinion is something that I can do more confidently. It's okay to voice an opinion. An opinion is not necessarily true or right, false or wrong – it's an opinion. Multiple opinions may be right at any one time. Plus, it's okay to be wrong.

There is one thing I'm certain about, and that's change. If we wait around for things to be right, certain or proved to be true, we'll be waiting a long time. And opinion will vary and change anyway, depending on circumstances, the environment and perspective. When you let go of the need to be right, all of a sudden you can be far more fearless in voicing your own opinion.

Letting go of the need to be in control

Not surprisingly, yet somewhat counter-intuitively, letting go of the need to be in control is empowering – although it's a far more common trait in feminine leadership. And I'm talking about *the need* to be in control with the emphasis on *need*. Remember the inclusive, collaborative characteristics where people are valued and relationships are nurtured? Yes, that's right – this is part and parcel of a feminine leadership style, and requires you to let go of the need to be in control.

Because there are so few iconic role models or success stories of leaders doing this well it's still challenging to understand. Our default mode and 'ideal' will likely be the masculine and bureaucratic leadership model that we see reinforced in the media, on television, in the movies and in the baby-boomer businessmen who still dominate our boardrooms around the globe – who appear to be *in control.* (Self-disclosure – I too am a Boomer).

Tony Hsieh of Zappos fame, an acknowledged introvert and successful entrepreneur who believes in challenging the status quo, provides a great example. Zappos, the online shoe store is (uniquely) most famous for selling happiness. He has also authored a book entitled *Delivering Happiness*. The Zappos customer care paradigm was, and still is, ground-breaking, with many companies now emulating their more humanised approach for both customers and staff. In a nutshell, they spent more money on customer service than on advertising, and grew their market share to the astonishment of all the experts.

More recently Zappos implemented a Holocractic management system (a flatter management structure), where hierarchical job titles were removed and replaced with a flatter "peer-to-peer operating system that increases transparency, accountability, and organisational agility."

While the Zappos story represents a fabulous case study, it's not the only one, and it takes my interpretation of letting go of the need to be in control to a whole new level. It is also a great example of how men are able to successfully embrace more feminised leadership principles with great success.

How does this apply to you?

- Instead of micromanaging your team and projects, allow your staff to have autonomy to succeed on their own, with the understanding that you are there to support if need be. Clear definitions of what success looks and feels like really help as well.

- Instead of feeling threatened when a talented staff member proposes an idea that's different or better than your own, embrace the new idea and champion the talent to see it through to fruition.

- Instead of feeling under attack by ambitious younger staff, and then working harder and harder yourself to try and make sure you also look good, understand that if this ambition is harnessed and nurtured well under your guidance, it will help both you and your team to succeed.

The Dark Side of Hard Work, Perfectionism and Likeability as Strategies to Get Ahead – Letting go of too good, too much and too nice.

This next section is a collection of three of my more popular blogs repurposed for the book. While you've already read some of the sentiments previously in the section on 'letting go', the three blogs that follow put it in context –and maybe you will be inspired to share to help a woman somewhere. In a nutshell – the old beliefs around hard work, likeability and doing this well, have a downside. If you are reliant on these three strategies then you will be disappointed. Creating a career requires so much more than this, yet we're still told the opposite.

Disillusioned

Exhausted **Perfect** Exploited
(Too good)

Hard work **Likable**
(Too much) (Too nice)

Expected

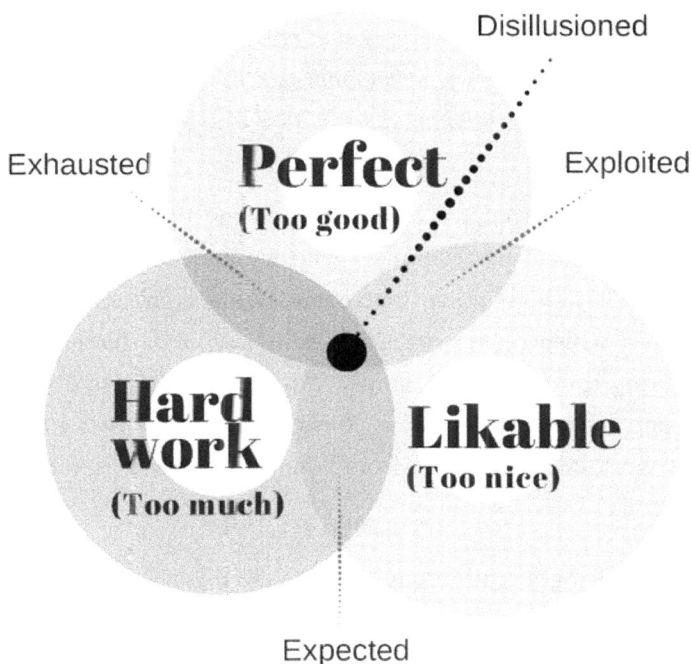

Blog 1: The Myth of Hard Work & How it Keeps us Playing Small

Much of my day is spent talking with women about how worn out they get;

- How they are tired of hitting their head up against road blocks, brick walls and glass ceilings

- How they are exhausted from striving for greatness and high achievement

- How they are worn out trying to have it all – you know, 'perfect house, perfect family, cook like a Masterchef and constant messages to #lookgoodnaked'.

> *"It feels good to give your unique and prestigious selves a slip every now and then and confess your membership in this unwieldy collective called the human race."* – Zadie Smith

I guess we need to accept a little of the blame though because we're frequently recovering perfectionists who try and do everything really, really well. That small voice that comes from somewhere near your shoulder that whispers messages of guilt, fear and shame and about not measuring up unless you simply work a little harder. It takes one to know one. That voice is/was a constant refrain for me. I blame my protestant work ethic but truly, from what I've seen, that voice is non-denominational.

But what if we've got it all wrong? Maybe there is another way. Perhaps our society's idolisation of, reliance on, and addiction to working hard, actually compounds inefficiency, causing us to miss out on opportunities for improvement, or simply masks real problems.

It's a bit like doing more and more cardio at the gym to help you lose weight. Yes, for some people it works – initially. And then you plateau. But we now know that there are a range of other (sometimes more) effective strategies to lose weight that also provide significant health benefits, that don't cause as much inflammation and, critically, don't leave us feeling worn out.

> *"So often people are working hard at the wrong thing. Working on the right thing is probably more important than working hard."*
> – Caterina Fake, Flickr co-founder

I'm tired of senior and seemingly successful men and women at industry conferences and networking events exhorting young professional and female audiences to work harder, and that hard work is all it takes. Perhaps this is because they had to work hard as young people and it appears to be human nature to want others to walk in our own footsteps, do the hard yards like we did.

So I've taken a stand. I know it's controversial, but I'm calling bullshit on this.

Working harder simply wears you out. Working harder is probably a key contributor in women *leaning out*. Remember how women tend to lose ambition after only two years? Remember too how we report to feeling more stressed and less confident than men?

From a purely business perspective, working harder disguises inefficiency, stifles innovation and it gets in the way of you getting ahead. No-one promotes the stressed out, flustered and exhausted person doing all the hard work up the back of the office with their head down to avoid trouble.

I know that everyone says they work hard and I suspect that's camouflage based on societal expectations. As women, we intuitively know that if we said that we got to where we wanted to go by taking it easy and hacking processes, we'd lose credibility and likeability in an instant. Yet we all know someone who made it to the corner office by way of corporate lunches, networking meetings and influence. It's not what you know; it's who you know, and how you let them know about you and your goals.

But is this different approach so wrong? What if business and society in general doesn't need more people working hard. Technology, outsourcing, automation and systems improvements remove this need. What we do need is more people making a bigger difference. Doing work you love doing, on projects that really matter for businesses, people and causes you believe in. And you may start seeing that you achieve far greater success than you thought possible – than when you simply worked hard.

Working hard is not all bad. In fact, there are times when hard work is a great strategy. However if it's your only strategy then you're in trouble. There is a finite cap on the amount of hard work a person can do, and unless you are part of that 15% of the population who thrive on very little sleep, then hard work is a diminishing resources as your energy reserves, motivation and health falter in the face of the constant grind.

Signs that you rely on hard work as a strategy

- You never have enough time to do everything you need

- You can barely afford the time to take holidays because there is so much to be done at work and at home

- You tell your kids that if they work hard they'll get ahead. This strategy worked back in the 50s and 60s but the nature of work has changed since then and smarter trumps harder almost every time

- You compliment the staff on how hard they work and send whole of staff emails to acknowledge those who stay late in the office (even in times of business as usual)

- Your language and metaphors are always about *knuckling down, noses to the grindstone* and *moving mountains*

- You rely on 'but we've always done it this way' because it's easier than thinking of a new way

- Your personal brand is all about *loyalty, hard work* and *relentless execution,* rather than that of *C-suite potential* or being the *talent in the leadership pipeline*

- You're the person people refer to when they say "give a busy woman something to do and she'll get it done"

- When asked about what your Unique Value Proposition is you tell people that you are hard-working, loyal and highly efficient

What can you do about it?

Recognition is the first step then doing something about it is next. Here are a range of tactics I suggest for my clients:

- Stop being busy, start being strategic

- Create your own game plan that nourishes you and sees you flourish and let go of the need to do everything and to please everyone

- Learn to prioritise with your career plan – ask yourself "What's the #1 thing I can do today that will move the dial on my career progress?", then do it

- When presented with a bunch of work to do or yet another late night at the office, pause a moment and ask why; "What is it that we're trying to achieve and is there a smarter way?"

- Learn to leverage your expertise, not your time – consider outsourcing, more efficient software solutions, asking for help, coaching and training others, an annual review of all procedures to see if there have been any new developments that would make processes more efficient and reduce effort

- Clean up your language and replace *efficient* with *effective*, and *work hard* with *work smart*

- Reframe your personal brand to focus on the language of value – *the difference you make the problems you solve and the value you add* – rather than *loyal, hard-working and dedicated*

- Next time you hear yourself say (out loud or mentally) "Give it to me, I'll do it", simply stop.

Why? Because on an individual level the cost of relying on hard work as your strategy to get ahead is way too high. At a collective level working harder is simply not getting us where we want to go. After all, we've been working hard at gender equality for many years and, despite huge effort by many, we haven't moved the dial very far very fast. It's high time we learned to work far smarter.

Blog 2: The Cost of Perfectionism

> *"Perfectionism is not the same thing as striving to be our best. Perfectionism is not about healthy achievement and growth; it's a shield."* – Brene Brown

For women there are two things that compete directly – perfectionism and having it all. In fact, perfectionism is one of the biggest hurdles in your journey to having it all! Counter-intuitively, perfectionism can be detrimental to you, your organisation and your role. It's damaging your career and your relationships. The cost of perfectionism is far too great for women – we need to learn another strategy.

I have a passion for yoga and teaching yoga. In some interpretations of yoga philosophy, perfectionism is seen as a form of violence – both towards yourself and others – and we are encouraged to let it go and practice 'getting messy on the mat'. But unless you carry that awareness with you off the yoga mat and into your daily life, it's challenging to keep this under control because doing things perfectly is so ingrained into the social expectations for women.

A couple of years ago, motivation expert, Dr Jason Fox mused hilariously about 'procrastifectionism' and oh, how it resonated. Procrastifectionism is the state of inertia caused by procrastinating AND being a perfectionist and can bring you to your knees, and is not limited to women.

The downsides of relying on perfectionism as a strategy to get ahead include:

- Resource blowouts of time, money and energy

- A sense of unworthiness or never feeling good enough

- Inertia and

- Lack of willingness to tackle things you aren't already good at.

Sound familiar?

Don't let perfect be the enemy of good

Here are four examples where perfectionism gets in the way;

- You have a project deadline that you miss, because you are still polishing up the details

- You have a critical deadline that you meet but it nearly kills you, because your perfectionist tendencies got in the way of finding a short cut or a more efficient solution

- Your first ever published article takes more than one month to refine – thereby delaying the launch of your business (oh right, that was me!)

- You don't apply for a role that looks great because you only meet three of the five criteria (yes, that's a reference to the Hewlett Packard internal report around gender differences in internal role applications).

The value of delivering average

Years ago I was challenged by a really smart manager to try and 'deliver average' every now and then, because it was not merely better for my own stress levels but also better for the business unit. While challenging to hear, it was probably the best career advice I've ever received. It was such a release to finally realise that I wasn't being paid to deliver perfect. I was being paid to deliver a result. After all, why deliver a Rolls Royce when the client has only paid for a Toyota?

Later on I remember being fascinated by a team that loved to deliver excellence – and yet their clients had only paid for a cheaper solution. In this instance:

- Perfectionism and striving for excellence were getting in the way of profitability

- Not only was this drive for 'excellence' costing the organisation to service the client, but it meant there was no room to move if and when a higher quality product was required

- Additionally, there was an opportunity cost – because everyone was so busy delivering the 'excellence' there was no-one out scouting about for new opportunities, or new development techniques, and staff were worn out all the time because they were on this continual never ending roller coaster ride of over delivering.

> *"If you don't take care of yourself, set your own standards, decide when enough is enough, learn to balance and rest, you'll have limited success. I learned that life was not about striving for perfection."*
>
> – Anita Krohn Traaseth

Rules of thumb

- Perfectionism is exhausting, unproductive, expensive, undermining and causes inertia – where effortless ease, confidence and a bias towards forward momentum, are far more helpful

- People promote those who deliver results, not simply for doing thing perfectly

- People rarely promote the worn out, strung out executive who delivers perfect because …. you look worn out and strung out all the time

- Organisations benefit in the short term by having people 'in the trenches' prepared to sacrifice their personal life for the good of the organisation without being asked, but in the long term, this is detrimental to sustainability

- The perfectionist runs the risk of finding themselves redundant as new innovative software solutions emerge that can deliver perfect with more precision, far faster and with less cost to the business

- Organisations of the future will require agile problem solvers, rather than those who can execute a procedure perfectly.

Some signs that you're a perfectionist

- Your work is never done because it's never quite good enough

- You're always putting finishing touches on items of work, despite deadlines past and potentially no-one else appreciating the additional quality anyway

- You feel resentful that no-one else in the office does quality work like you do

- You hate feedback and the annual performance appraisal sends you into a spiral of self-doubt and anxiety

- You never ask for anything if rejection is a possibility

- You are frequently last to leave the office yet not always the most productive

- You re-read your sent emails

- You send out group emails and then send another one shortly after to apologise and correct a relatively minor typo

- You're more worried about what other people will think of you rather than the people you can help with the work you do

- When someone else makes a mistake it's okay and you are forgiving, but if you make a mistake, the negative self-talk lasts for days

- You whinge about those who seem to have more career success than you yet all they seem to do is go out to lunch, schmooze and are never in the office doing the actual work

- You're secretly competitive about the quality of your output so if there is any chance you won't compare as well you keep your work hidden

- You don't like trying new things where you will obviously fail.

Notice I did not list having a tidy desk, having a tidy house, or having it all together. I've even heard people who are in perfectionist denial saying that they couldn't be a perfectionist because they have a messy desk/ spare room/car/haven't done their tax yet. The perfectionist may have a few things that they've decided they can let slide (despite suppressing shame, fear and guilt) but then there are a bunch of things that are the non-negotiable, where ego simply won't allow them to deliver average on.

What can you do about it?

Recognise the signs. Of course there will be times when quality control is paramount. But if your perfectionist tendencies are getting in the way of your career success, recognition of your C-suite goals, or even taking time away from your personal life, then it's time to address the problem. Try some of the following:

- Embrace Stamford Professor Carol Dweck's 'growth mindset' – where you understand that your abilities, capabilities and IQ can grow

- Learn to deliver average at strategic times – and understand that some people choose to deliver average all the time because it costs less to them personally. In an environment where quality control is paramount, have systems and processes in place to mitigate risk

- Embrace the notion of failure practice – where you deliberately learn new things that are well outside of your natural talents and abilities. I'm a big fan of learning to slack-line (like tight rope walking but on a loose rope) – because it's uncontrollable, unpredictable and extremely difficult to get right the first time – plus it's huge fun

- Play the rejection game – where you reframe the notion of getting rejection into a challenge, so that you become more likely to ask for things where 'no' is a possible answer. After all, the more no's you get, the closer you are to a yes

- And start collecting evidence of wins, achievements and successes including the small stuff. Frequently a perfectionist is so busy aiming for perfect on big things that they (we) need to be reminded to stop and smell the roses. The world won't fall apart if the bed is not made, your report has an error in it, or you behave less than ideally in that meeting with your team. But it might if you have to take time off for stress leave after aiming for an impossibly perfect future.

Blog 3: The Curse of Likeability

"Well-behaved women seldom make history." – Laurel Thatcher Ulrich

I read quotes like that of the famous line from Laurel Thatcher Ulrich and am inspired, in awe and totally on board. Yet when the rubber hits the road, I'm the first to admit that in the past I've chosen to be liked over being remembered for my achievements. I've even made decisions about my own career that have been motivated by my need to be liked. For example, when I found a role that was ideal for both me and my friend (peer) that we were both eminently qualified for and neither of us applied because we didn't want to damage the friendship. Possibly on a purely social measure, this was the right decision, but surely if the friendship was an honest and open one there would be alternatives.

While the need to be loved or liked is be part of the human condition, I suspect that women have been socialised to need be liked far more than men and it's become the social norm. We trade on likeability – it makes it easier for us to achieve things or get ahead if we're seen as likeable. It's also expected of us.

But in the workplace, creating a personal brand that combines likeability and getting things done is a delicate balance. If we're too likeable we're considered ineffective – it's a liability, a burden and a curse all in one. Yet if we get it wrong there is a large social cost which is far greater for women than for men. When we behave in less than stereotypically feminine ways we bear the burden:

- You may have heard of Facebook COO, Sheryl Sandberg, and her #banbossy campaign – which highlighted that when a young girl is direct and forthright we label her bossy yet if a young boy behaves that same way he's merely developing his leadership potential

- When women negotiate too hard we're labelled as hard-nosed or aggressive if on behalf of someone else, and greedy if on behalf of ourselves. While men also bear some social cost it's far greater for a woman, with aggressiveness and money orientation seen as a more stereotypically masculine traits anyway

- When we talk about our own wins and achievements we are perceived as displaying naked self-promotion, yet it's okay for a man to do the same

- When we need to give feedback or are required to performance manage someone we worry about their feelings (displaying emotional intelligence) because if we don't we're labelled not nice or hard-nosed (with the inference being that nice is better than effective) plus there is the lasting legacy of hurt feelings and remembered pain.

If and when we act feminine enough, which includes being inclusive and concerned about the wellbeing of others, then we win in the likeability stakes. When we behave in less than stereotypically feminine ways we worry about losing in the likeability stakes – and with valid concerns.

"The research could not be more clear in that we tolerate more aggressive or assertive behaviour by men more than women."

– Linda Babcock

However, I also believe that some women (me included) can take *this need to be liked* to another level. As a regular *people pleaser* from way back, putting other people's needs before my own, worrying about what other people think and waiting for the approval of others, have each been significant stumbling blocks. I've always operated with the mantra of 'you can attract more flies with honey' as a strategy, yet as a career strategy it gets in the way.

"If you just set out to be liked, you will be prepared to compromise on anything at any time, and would achieve nothing."

– Margaret Thatcher

Some signs that you're focused too much on likeability

- Not wanting to express a controversial opinion

- Struggling to provide feedback without over polite qualifiers

- Worrying about other people's feelings and needs before your own

- Avoiding difficult conversations at all costs

- Avoiding making decisions until you've got consensus from everyone involved

- Hating performance appraisal time because you take the criticism as a personal criticism

- Struggling to performance manage or provide constructive feedback to staff

- Martyring yourself to protect your staff

- Engaging in people pleasing behaviours such as trying to curry favour or buy approval i.e. you baked muffins for the 80 head office staff

- Prefacing opinions with "I'm no expert but…"

- Under-negotiating on behalf of yourself or your team

- Not being able to separate your identity from your performance

- Worrying about how other people perceive you so your own sense of identity is compromised

- Focusing on looking pretty, young and appealing rather than credible – and there's some really fun research available about how looking young and feminine gets in the way of perceptions about your competence and influence. See:

    https://blog.photofeeler.com/gender-bias-study/

What can you do about it?

Once again recognition is the first step then action is key. And while the delicate balance between 'nice girl' and 'hard-nosed b*tch' is challenging to navigate, it's not impossible. Yes, we live in a biased world and some of what I say may not seem fair, but if your goal is get a seat at the table so that we can change the way things are then maybe we need to learn. Remember, we want the trifecta – to be paid well (and equally), to have a voice and to make a bigger difference. Learning to navigate the likeability honey pot is key.

- If your journey is a leadership journey, stop trying to look young and pretty and focus instead on appearing credible, influential and leaderly. Young and pretty does buy likeability, but depending on your industry and target audience, doesn't necessarily buy credibility and influence – the currency of your leadership aspirations

- Update your LinkedIn photo and any web presence with a photo that positions you as a credible expert, rather than cute or funny

- Learn how to have difficult conversations

- Learn to make decisions on your own – and remember Maggie Thatcher

- Make a weekly habit of collecting and quantifying evidence of wins and achievements so that you can articulately quantify or defend performance debates if required rather than be perceived as bragging – great if you've been criticised for being aggressive when all you've done is led a change management program and stood your ground on a few issues that challenged the old guard

- Learn to separate your work performance from your identity – a project failure is not a criticism of your personal identity – and as someone wisely said to me, her business failure was better than any MBA

- Find your *why*. Once you find your why it is far easier to be yourself and do the work you need to do, whether you are liked or not.

Chapter 5

Fear, Doubt
and Low Confidence

Step Up
Speak Out
Take Charge

Chapter 5

Fear, Doubt and Low Confidence

The Irrationality of Fear

When we think about fear most of us are simply imagining the emotion or perhaps the last time we experienced it. We are most likely thinking of the last time we experienced a gut wrenching shock or a life-threatening experience. In this situation we experience what's called the Amygdala Hijack – where the amygdala, the part of our brain that registers a fear situation, tries to get us out of trouble, fast. It reacts in the absence of rational thought, with the intent of keeping us safe by bypassing the rational parts of our brain and reacting incredibly fast with what's called the fight, flight or freeze response.

In our daily lives though, we experience a range of other emotions that are closely linked to fear. In fact, according to author Taylor Clark in his book *Nerve*, stress, anxiety and worry are all part of the fear bucket of emotions.

What happens when we become overwhelmed with our daily grind? Picture this - you're stressed at work because of project deadlines, the end of financial year is looming and you have some big targets, plus there is a performance management situation you need to take care of. Then something happens at home that triggers you to worry about the kids or your partner, and you start anxiously anticipating situations that may or may not occur, simply because you've become hyper-sensitive.

Upon reflection you can see that you aren't acting rationally. Your autonomic fear response is trying keep you safe – by helping you avoid danger, get out of dangerous situations faster or by stopping you from doing something dangerous. Unfortunately this response is not great at differentiating between all the different things that are triggering your stress and/or fear response – so it treats them all the same.

When we're scared, stressed, anxious and worried we run the risk of our brain responding by bypassing more rational thought processes, making it more challenging to make great decisions.

Perception is the key

Your mind also doesn't really discern much of a difference between threat of pain to person and threat of pain to ego. The pain centres of the brain light up in the same place when you hurt yourself or when someone 'unfriends' you on Facebook. We even avoid threats to ego with as much energy as we avoid threats to physical self – perhaps explaining why (according to comedian Jerry Seinfeld) most of us are more afraid of giving the eulogy at a funeral than being in the casket.

Why is this important? If your fear response is triggered by ambiguity, uncertainty and the unknown, you may not be perceiving the situation accurately or rationally.

Let's get some of the most common fears out in the open so you can recognise them and let them go when you start moving past dreams into execution phase.

1. Fear of failure

> *"Success is not final; failure is not fatal: it is the courage to continue that counts."* – Winston Churchill

Many of us appear to imagine that initially not succeeding at something is an end point. And yet our society reveres stories that celebrate learning from repeated failures – such as the invention of the 'post-it' note, Thomas Edison's 10,000 attempts to invent the light globe – and the good old fashioned 'try, try again' approach.

When was the last time you tried something you were bound to fail at first? Probably not since you were a child.

Introducing Failure Practice: Why not try something really out of the box that you are bound to fail at on first attempt? Go do something that you know that you'll be lousy at and see how it actually feels (not how you imagine it feels like). Instead of making excuses or justifying afterwards, let it happen. Enjoy the 'experience' of not being perfect and either try again or move on. My personal recommendation for those who are able bodied, is to try slack lining as you've read previously. It's virtually impossible to get right the first time and requires a huge degree of being able to deal with uncertainty and almost certain initial failure.

> *"I have not failed, I have just found 10,000 ways that won't work."*
>
> – Thomas Edison

2. Fear that people will find out that you are a fraud (Imposter Syndrome)

> *"Any moment someone's going to find out I'm a total fraud – I can't possibly live up to what everyone thinks I am."* – Emma Watson

If Emma Watson can experience Imposter Syndrome, then it must be okay for the rest of us mere mortals to experience it. Imposter Syndrome is where you find yourself out of your depth, doubting yourself, your credibility and your ability and in a nutshell, feeling like a fraud. Certainly if you are worn out, under pressure and out of your comfort zone, you will be more susceptible. It's a very real syndrome but once again, not fatal. Nearly every one (men and women) experience it at some stage in their career. Identify it, take a moment, then move through it.

> *"Both men and women suffer from it in different ways, but it does affect both sexes ... With women they are more likely to be afraid of success – as well as failure – because they sense there will be a price to pay in other parts of their life ...With men it is more 'fake it, until you make it'. They think the syndrome is part and parcel of work life and they tend to push through it."*
>
> – Suzanne Mercier, behavioural change consultant

3. Fear that you won't like it when you get there

Embedded in this fear is the idea that there is a 'there' or end point. Surely life, success, career and adventures are a big continuum? If perception is everything, why not extend your end point so that you've still got something enjoyable to aim for? Then refer back to fear # 1.

> *"Success is not final."* – Winston Churchill

Elon Musk, serial entrepreneur, once famously likened the pathway to entrepreneurial success to eating glass. Many would agree that the pathway towards success as an entrepreneur or leader is not easy. Be clear about what you are looking for. Something easy? A challenge? To make a difference? Do your homework – what is important to you about work? Once you are clear about that, it will be far easier to like when you get there.

4. Fear of being great

> *"Our deepest fear is not that we are inadequate. Our deepest fear is that we are powerful beyond measure. It is our light, not our darkness that most frightens us. We ask ourselves, who am I to be brilliant, gorgeous, talented, fabulous?"* – Marianne Williamson

I've had clients as they start their journey with me share that they are worried how they may change if and when they 'shine' and that it will negatively impact their relationship with their family or significant other – hence hesitation or stalling. Fair enough. So why not stop worrying about it, and work it though instead? Journal it, have a conversation with your significant other. Work it through with a '45 why' process (page 122). Then put some plans, routines and certainty in place to nurture those relationships in advance. To paraphrase an old proverb:

> *"Worry is like a rocking chair. It gives you something to do but it doesn't get you anywhere."*

5. Fear that you won't be enough

> *"Whether you think you can or you think you can't – you're right."*
> *– Henry Ford*

The ailment and the remedy in one wise statement above. If you think you are enough or you think you aren't enough, you will be right. But fear of not being good enough is deeply ingrained for many. Once again, the fix similar to those who experience Imposter Syndrome. Take a break, then put one foot in front of the other to get through.

If you are prone to low self-esteem, low confidence and self-doubt, then I highly recommend keeping a confidence journal. Inside your confidence journal keep notes of your daily gratitude practice, along with capturing your wins and achievements at the end of the day. Then on a weekly basis, document, describe and quantify your big wins, along with the expertise required to achieve those wins. Make this part of your non-negotiable routine. Systematise your pathway to success as much as possible and don't underestimate the power of mindset.

6. Fear of not being loved

This is probably the biggest and most common of all fears and truly gets in the way of being great. The fear of not being loved drives us to take risks, behave in odd ways, feel resentful and lash out unlovingly amongst other things – all counter-productive to being loved. Yet we all do it. What is it about the human condition that makes us contrary?

> *"A deep sense of love and belonging is an irreducible need of all people. We are biologically, cognitively, physically, and spiritually wired to love, to be loved, and to belong. When those needs are not met, we don't function as we were meant to. We break. We fall apart. We numb. We ache. We hurt others. We get sick."*
>
> – Brene Brown

Without heading too much into 'woo woo' territory, self-love is probably the best medicine. Learn to love yourself. When we are able to love ourselves unconditionally, we are far more generous with our affections to others. Yet generosity is the key here. Feeling a little unloved? Why not switch this around?

- Tell your best friend how much you enjoy their company and watch their face light up with appreciation and they may even reciprocate

- Acknowledge that your staff don't turn up to work aiming to do bad work. Instead tell them about the things that they are doing well, and see their performance improve, plus they're more likely to show you appreciation in return

- In fact, why not implement an *appreciative enquiry* process at work as an initiative to identify and drive great performance

- Instead of nit-picking at your significant other when you're stressed and anxious, identify all the things you love about them, tell them and see that love returned, which will in turn help you manage your stress and anxiety better.

Love, generosity and happiness truly are unbounded resources when we allow. By being afraid of being loved yourself, you are probably cutting off the one precious resource you need most. Go on, love a little. You know you want to.

7. Fear that it won't work and you'll have wasted your time and energy

This idea is predicated on a model of scarcity. That time, energy and confidence will run out if you don't shepherd them carefully. I know this one intimately. I've lived with this for over a decade. It keeps you at home on the couch ostensibly restoring – but instead depleting.

But what if you believe instead that energy breeds energy, that action boosts confidence and that time feels abundant as soon as you allow yourself to realise it's not running out?

At some level we know deep down that these fears are irrational. We also know that when we are overwhelmed, overworked and feeling stressed, perceived fear has far more impact. Be sure to keep your *eyes on the prize* and focused on the end goal. Put systems, processes and routines in place that keep you supported physically and mentally, allowing you to tackle big, important, career and entrepreneurial goals while managing your perceptions of fear more easily.

Ask yourself:

- What are you afraid of?

- What holds you back?

- What stops you from executing big, audacious goals?

- What can we learn so that others don't need to go through the same?

- What have I got to lose? And perhaps more importantly …

- What have I got to lose if I don't?

"The key to success is to focus our conscious mind on things we desire, not things we fear." – Brian Tracy

---

Confidence

There is a strong argument that women appear to be less confident than men. Perhaps, from an evolutionary perspective, our brains are wired to scan the environment for threats so we can metaphorically protect the offspring in our care while the men are off hunting metaphorical woolly mammoths – ergo we are less confident in scenarios that feel threatening. Katty Kay and Claire Shipman's book *The Confidence Code: The Science and Art of Self-Assurance – What Women Should Know* is a must read for women everywhere.

While I don't pretend to know if the science they uncover is true or not (certainly I've met some amazingly confident women and equally some less than confident men) the stereotypical role model differences for men and women see women playing a less than confident game. Women are far more likely to report feeling less than confident compared to men especially in arenas that are stereotypically designated as masculine – such as leadership.

Underestimation

You've read already about the research that indicates women tend to underestimate their performance while men tend to overestimate theirs. Yet when researchers measure actual performance, we perform the same. For example, if you were asked to rate yourself on a scale of one to ten in terms of your ability to do something like maths. If you are a woman you'd be more likely to rate yourself a six. If you were a man you may rate yourself an eight or a nine. When the results are in we all perform at about seven and a half (or thereabouts).

Unfortunately, the flow-on effect of underestimation in that we frequently don't stretch as far or as high as is possible for us, which goes some way to precluding us from meatier and more substantive opportunities. It may also mean we're less likely to put our hand up for things where there is more competition.

Tara Mohr, in *Playing Big*, challenged the assumption that low confidence was behind the Hewlett Packard *gender differences in internal promotions* research previously mentioned. Her own research found that women were less likely to apply if we didn't think we'd be in the running, if it wasn't part of the game, and we didn't want to waste anyone's time including our own.

You've also read about the new study by researchers at the University of Michigan that backs this up finding that that women tend to shy away from opportunities where there is more competition.

Here are a few things that I've discovered in the literature that may contribute to you feeling less than confident, less competitive or less likely to throw your hat in the ring, even as you begin to 'lean in' at work or into tackling goals outside of your comfort zone.

1. **Hormones** – and I'm not talking about monthly hormonal swings that appear to get the blame for everything including emotion, feeling flustered and/or hot and bothered. I'm talking specifically about hormonal differences that possibly impact on someone feeling less than confident.

    a) *Testosterone* – we know that is a hormone that is about ten times higher in men than women. It is a hormone that inspires action, risk taking and competitiveness. You can bet your bottom dollar that not being so inspired will contribute to feelings of lower confidence in situations that require action, risk taking and competitiveness - or in masculine dominated environments.

    b) *Oestrogen* – higher in women than in men and a hormone that promotes connection and bonding. On the flipside, this hormone appears to discourage conflict and risk-taking. You can certainly understand that when a woman is 'competing' in a male dominated field these differences in hormones will have some impact and contribute to feelings of being different or feeling less than confident.

    Interestingly in research conducted in 2012 by the Wellcome Trust Centre for Neuroimaging at UCL (University College London), women who were given testosterone were less able to collaborate, wrong more often and behaved more egocentrically. Be careful what you wish for.

Simply understanding these differences will help you navigate those uncertain feelings more easily. When you are watching a male peer perform more aggressively, assertively and far more confidently, this doesn't mean he is likely to be more right or more accurate. Simply that due to biological and socialisation differences he acts more confidently – and you could do the same. In a society that values high confidence and rates those who behave more confidently with higher social prominence – then this understanding is critical.

2. **Anxiety and worry** – the punishment for having a brain that is good at identifying risk, is having a brain that is good at identifying risk. Did you know that, according to fear researchers, women are twice as likely to experience anxiety and worry as men? Certainly women are far more likely to report to those feelings.

    a) *The amygdala* which we read about earlier in the chapter, which is seated at the base of the brain, scans for risk and is usually known in relation to triggering our fear responses of flight, fight or freeze. It's affectionately nicknamed the lizard brain as it is really not linked to rational thought at all. And here's the difference – Functional magnetic resonance imaging (fMRI) indicates that women trigger the fear response more easily than men, we also feel negative fear emotions more strongly than men, and those emotions create longer lasting memories. Fight, flight or freeze are great responses in the face of spiders, snakes and oncoming out of control trucks, but not great in the boardroom where for whatever reason your amygdala may be feeling hyper-sensitive.

    b) *The anterior cingulate cortex* is another small part of the brain that constantly scans for risk – a little like a virus scanner on your laptop. Its nickname is the 'worrywart centre'. You can no doubt see where this particular argument leads. In many women the worrywart centre grows to about twice the size as in men.

It would appear that women are (or become) finely tuned to assess and scan for risk, which is great from an evolutionary perspective, and also leads to the different risk profiles in male and female investors – with women being commonly known to make far better investors in the long term. Recently Catherine Robson, CEO of Affinity Private, The Age's 'Money Brain' columnist and women's leadership podcast host has published an article entitled *Warren Buffett Invests Like a Girl – why women are investment naturals.* (I take this as a compliment.) So the flipside of being more cautious is that we make better investors. Yet does this risk focus also contribute to women feeling less than confident and less inclined to decisiveness, risk taking or action in the face of uncertainty?

3. **Resilient boys** – one of the theories is that we bring up young boys to be more resilient in the face of adversity - which highlights the impact of nurturing differences. When a young boy falls over in the playground, as parents we are more likely to pick him up, dust him off and push him back out there into the rough and tumble. On the other hand, when a young girl falls over in the playground we are less likely to do the same. In fact, the traditional role of parenting is to protect our young girls. Does this grow resilient boys more able to act in the face of adversity? I'm not sure. I'm not a parent so not qualified to comment. However, there is no disputing the fact that our western cultures are protective of young girls and far more likely to encourage boys to 'get over it' and get on back out there with the other guys.

4. **Imposter Syndrome** – Yes, we all face it at times. We've already addressed that in the section on Fear. And, because corporate work is still structured around typically masculine notions and hierarchical structures, with fewer women in senior leadership roles the higher up the ranks you go, women experience Imposter Syndrome more than men.

I remember experiencing a severe case of Imposter Syndrome some years ago after a particularly hard financial year where we only barely scraped through to deliver a surplus for the organisation. At the time I was working with a business coach and I mentioned to him that I thought I was in over my head, that I had nothing left, should resign and that I really wasn't the right person for the role. This was despite the fact that we had returned a surplus for the third year in a row, in the face of a tough period in the organisation. Anyone would have found it tough going.

My coach at the time, who had no real understanding of what I was going through because he had never really experienced it, simply advised "time to take a holiday". And while now I know what I was experiencing and why, it was great advice. I needed a rest, to regroup and recalibrate in order to prepare for the next period of digging deep.

You can imagine my surprise when reading about the issues that men and women face at work I came across Imposter Syndrome. Why isn't this mandatory teaching at university?

And after reading a fascinating interview about Christine Lagarde, head of the IMF – who confided to Katty Kay and Claire Shipman of *The Confidence Code* that when she felt overwhelmed from over-preparing because she was nervous of being caught out, she rang her buddy Angela Merkel (Chancellor of Germany) – all of a sudden I felt in great company and less unusual. My rationale? If Christine and Angela can feel like this at times and have strategies to mitigate – then it's okay for the rest of us to deal with Imposter Syndrome on occasion.

5. **Social cost** – specifically the social cost (where people like you less) of being successful. Here in Australia we even have a name for it and we call it 'Tall Poppy Syndrome'. Anyone who sticks their head up above the crowd, does things differently or positions herself or

himself as a leader, becomes a target for criticism.

Women face even stronger social penalties that include being criticised by both men and women for behaving in less than socially accepted ways for women. Tell people how well you are doing in a slightly less than feminine way, and it's considered to be bragging. Negotiate hard on your own behalf and you'll face the brunt of a legacy of social stigma amongst those who know. Use a show of strength to drive change or act decisively in the workplace – and you're opening yourself up to be criticised as aggressive again. Women know this innately. We've been brought up with this since we were little girls. We know we need to walk that fine line in order to get things done where likeability is the trade-off if you 'play' as aggressively as your male peers.

Bias, both conscious and unconscious, is ingrained into our social blueprint. We expect both men and women to behave in certain ways. If a woman talks about her wins and successes too much like a man, she bears the risk of criticism. The flipside is also true for men – if a man talks about his success too much like a woman then he will be criticised.

We all know a female leader somewhere who appears to have clambered up the leadership ladder by acting in fairly masculine ways - and yet we might secretly criticise her. We all know women who have expressed their ambitions to run multimillion dollar empires, who have been silently undermined on a social level.

Social cost is alive and well. Societies the world over are nervous with anyone who doesn't fit the stereotype. So does this then contribute to us from sharing those stories and making it far more normal? And does this in turn lead to women appearing as though they are less than confident.

Chapter 6

The Power of Mindset

Step Up
Speak Out
Take Charge

Chapter 6

The Power of Mindset

"We like to think of our champions and idols as superheroes who were born different from us. We don't like to think of them as relatively ordinary people who made themselves extraordinary."

– Carol Dweck,
Mindset: The New Psychology of Success

Have you ever noticed that successful people tackle big challenges and opportunities really differently? When approached with a new idea or big opportunity, they will frequently say "Hell yes, of course I can", then work out how to do it afterwards. And yet much of the rest of the population are far more likely to demur until they feel better prepared.

In my reading around leadership, some of the challenges that women face in their career journeys and success stories from those who are already doing it, there is one common factor and that's mindset. Leaders, entrepreneurs and those who we consider to be successful all focus on mindset.

Mindset is key and whether our mindset is dictated by socialisation or genetics, no-one is really sure, but given the amazing neuroplasticity of the brain, changing how we think and act is definitely an option. Remember, just because you think and behave a certain way, doesn't mean you always have to think and behave a certain way.

The growth vs fixed mindset

Dr Carol Dweck, of Stanford University, introduced the concept of fixed and growth mindsets – with the fixed mindset where you believe your abilities, your capabilities and your IQ are fixed or capped in some way. Maybe you did an IQ test at school and you thought that your IQ was a finite resource or you were told that you weren't good at maths or art. If you have a fixed mindset then you won't bother trying when faced with a maths or art challenge, because you believe you simply can't do anything about it.

If you have a growth mindset on the other hand, you understand that your abilities, capabilities and IQ are pliable, can expand and increase with learning, challenge and stimulation. This growth mindset means you can virtually tackle anything you choose to tackle, you can do almost anything you put your mind to, as long as you are prepared:

- to make mistakes,

- to be distinctly uncomfortable

- to do the work.

What does this mean? This is the premise of the wonderful Henry Ford quote:

"If you think you can, or you think you can't, you are right."

It's possible to have a mix of both mindsets. When I look back at my own career there were things that I found easy. I believed that those were the things that I should be doing more of and that I probably shouldn't waste my time on things that I wasn't naturally good at.

Interestingly, spring forward 20 years and I now speak and write for a living – two things that I would never have said I was naturally good at. But when you adopt a growth mindset, you realise that you can tackle almost anything you choose, should you choose.

What mindset will be more helpful in your leadership journey? What's going to bring your future self far closer far faster? Fixed or growth? You decide.

Agile learning – closely linked with having a growth mindset

While not exactly mindset, another characteristic of leaders is the ability to learn on the fly. Entrepreneurs and leaders tend to be more agile learners. They understand that just-in-time learning is equally as valid (if not more) as old school learning. The ability to be agile represents the 'ability to respond quickly to the fast pace of change' in your market or area – and to learn from experience without becoming rigid. Agile learning also has an aspect of emotional intelligence and responsiveness. According to research by Korn Ferry:

> *"Companies with the most agile learners among their executive ranks have profit margins 25% higher than those of other, similar companies."*

Interestingly, female entrepreneurs trump C-suite executives when it comes to agile learning according to an Inc. article entitled *Why Women Entrepreneurs Make the Best Leaders.*

Most girls are very good at navigating the education system. We get great grades, we keep out of trouble and we, mostly, love going to school – compared to boys. We are even over-represented in postgraduate education with statistics indicating that women make up about 62% of post graduate students in Australia. But being good at formal education is not translating into leadership roles or equal salary.

Carol Dweck says it all.

> *"If life were one long grade school, women would be the undisputed*
> *rulers of the world"*

But it's not.

I'm not saying don't go to university. But I am saying that relying on formal education as a fast track for your career and leadership aspirations is a flawed notion. You *also* need to have a swathe of other tools in your tool belt. We're in a world that values technology and speed, so things are getting faster and changing ever more rapidly even in the span of a few years. Your ability to learn agilely is going to become increasingly important.

A possibility mindset

A possibility mindset means that when a new idea is presented, you see a range of possibilities potentially available – options, variations, a light at the end of the tunnel – rather than all the things that could go wrong. It's a bit like having rose-tinted glasses. And the good thing? Recent research is proving that this type of positive thinking, seeing the good, not that bad, actually changes your brain in positive ways. In fact, it's entirely possible to change yourself from being a pessimist to an optimist in only eight weeks.

When we're healthy, happy and feel certain, a possibility mindset is easy to adopt. On the flipside when we're feeling stressed, overwhelmed and overworked, we're far more likely to reject possibility and put up road blocks. Uncertainty is a huge trigger for roadblocks.

Picture this – a stay at home mum who in a previous life had been a copywriter. She was bored but more importantly wanted to bring in an income stream to help look after her family. So she became what's called a 'professional comper'. Professional comper I hear you ask? Yes. Professional comper. She used her copy writing skills to go in lots of competitions that asked for a response "in 25 words or less" or thereabouts. If and when she won a prize (and she won a few), then she would auction the winnings off on EBay. Now don't quote me, but I heard that she was bringing in $60K per annum doing this, give or take.

This is a great example of how valuable having a possibility mindset is. The woman had more legitimate excuses for not getting out of her rut than most. She:

- Had small children and couldn't leave the house (roadblock) – so she solved that by working from home (possibility)

- Couldn't work regular hours in an office (roadblock) – so she did her work at any time of day or night (possibility)

- Didn't really need the prize-winnings (roadblock) – so she sold them on eBay and turned her winnings into things she did like (possibility)

- Didn't win anything at first (roadblock) – so it became a numbers game and an opportunity for growth until she developed enough skill and technique to win enough prizes to bring in a reasonable income (possibility).

- Didn't want to do this for the rest of her life (roadblock) – but used it as a springboard for down the track when she had more personal freedom (possibility).

Why is this important? Because when you're heading into the uncertain terrain, it's going to be easy to see all the things that could possibly go wrong. Instead of automatically responding to those negative thoughts, why not choose to question them? Or explore the flipside and see if the opposite is not also true.

To paraphrase a common saying – if you're pigeonholing yourself as a glass half empty person or a glass half full person you are missing the point. The glass is refillable!

Let go of all or nothing thinking and always thinking

As important as adopting a growth mindset, agile learning practices and a possibility mindset, so too is letting go of other mindsets that aren't helpful.

When I'm working with clients, depending on where they are up to in their own personal journey, I sometimes hear a lot of "that's not possible for me", or "I don't know how to do that", or "that's fine for some people to afford, but not for me".

Recently I attended a conference to inspire female entrepreneurs. While I thoroughly enjoyed the lessons shared by amazing entrepreneurial women, I was taken aback by the response by one or two of my fellow attendees. Picture this – your new entrepreneurial conference buddy is talented, skilled and passionate about her area of work and is thinking about setting up her own business. She mentions that that the work of one of the speakers in the NFP space really inspired her, but when we asked if she too could work in that area, she said "No, because I'll never be able to do it as well as what's already out there, so I'll not do it at all".

Her 'all or nothing' thinking (if I can't do it well I won't do it at all) closed off any possibility that there was another opportunity worth exploring.

At the same event I was speaking with yet another attendee about successful social media strategies and referring to one of the speaker's use of Instagram – and the comment from this attendee was, "Well Instagram works for them because they are a fashion label, it will never work for me like that". In this instance it was 'always thinking' (a milder form of catastrophising) closed off any possibility that there were any transferable lessons or insights despite the differences in products.

In both instances the individual may have been right, but the dominant negative thought patterns of 'always', 'never' or 'if I can't do it well I won't do it at all' definitely means these individuals won't even give it a try or bother to explore. My new friend who was wary of Instagram will never find out whether or not it will work because her mindset closed her off to even finding out how to use Instagram in other ways.

Beware automatic negative thoughts (ANTs)

Dr Daniel Amens is the author of several books including *Unleash the Power of the Female Brain*. In some of his earlier writing he talks about ANTS – Automatic Negative Thinking and the examples above are classic.

All or nothing thinking – it's either all in or all out, there is no mid-ground. This really fits in with the perfectionist tendencies – "If I can't do something properly or well, then I won't do it at all".

How on earth did you learn to drive? We certainly didn't come out of the womb knowing how to walk and talk already. Most importantly this way of thinking yet again, keeps us playing small and safe where adopting a growth mindset would definitely be more helpful.

Dramatic language is a dead giveaway

Look for dramatic language such as:

- "My boss *always* micromanages me."
- "My team are *always* late in the morning."
- "My *whole* business is failing because we didn't win that client."
- "This *entire* report is rubbish because of the typo near the beginning."
- "I'm *always* dreadfully unhappy in the winter."

- "My husband *never* puts the dishes in the dishwasher even when I ask him."

- "If I can't do the 90-minute yoga class, then I'm not going to *any* at all."

If you've noticed this type of pattern start questioning yourself – are you actually right? Or is it that you have simply become used to using dramatic language and it's now shaping your behaviour? Surely 30 to 60 minutes of exercise is better than no exercise? There are probably even days in winter when it rains and you are happy or likely only mildly miserable. The dramatic phrasing is a dead giveaway.

With regard to career goals – 'all or nothing' thinking will definitely keep you playing a much smaller game.

- "If I can't land that promotion easily then I won't even bother applying."

- "I'll never be as good as (insert incumbent's name) so I won't waste anyone's time in even going for it."

- "I didn't think they would appoint me since I didn't meet all the criteria, and I didn't want to waste my time and energy."

- "There was a bullet point in the job advertisement that I don't meet so I won't bother applying"

Combine 'all or nothing' thinking along with a dose of perfectionism and you are well on the way to playing (and staying) small.

The way we do anything is the way we do everything

There is a saying – the way we do anything is the way we do everything. It means that the way we think and react in any situation is the way we think and react in nearly every situation. So what else are you missing out on because of all or nothing thinking, unwillingness to embrace agile learning as a discipline or you have a fixed mindset? If this is you then it's time to audit your thinking to help you get ahead more easily.

Signs that you need to change your mindset or change your mind

- When you're looking for that idea for your next career move and you ask your friends for ideas, only to shut down nearly every idea that they provide

- When you get frustrated that your mentor seems to be only giving you 'stupid' ideas when you ask for help on your next career move

- When you look enviously at someone else making bold audacious career moves and think 'well it's okay for them' with the inference it's not okay for you

- When you look at someone else's success and think 'How on earth did they do that? I'm far smarter than them. It must have been luck'.

- When you tell someone that their idea will never work only to find out in a year that they've done it successfully – despite your feedback

To quote an old Chinese proverb

> *"People who say it cannot be done, should not interrupt those already doing it."*

See Limitations as Challenges – take charge of the narrative

In Tasmania there used to be a traffic speed sign that always made me laugh... It was a 100km per hour speed sign and it has a tagline that says "This is a limit, not a challenge".

It was a great reminder that you don't have to actually get up to 100km per hour if it feels unsafe.

However, when it comes to career and progress the opposite applies. The same safety precautionary measures aren't required. In fact, I'm giving you permission to take off the handbrake and aim to break the limit instead. Some of the most successful people I know see limitations as a challenge and that is the thing that separates them from others.

Examples

- Speaking – maybe you present at a conference and do a lousy job. Instead of seeing this as a limitation, accept the challenge of improving. Accept that this was the starting point on your journey. An inspiring woman I know had exactly this experience. She delivered an industry conference presentation that received average ratings and she was extremely disappointed. Yet she used it as a learning experience and … made her debut on the TEDx stage a few years later. She saw the poor speaking as something she could overcome and the poor feedback galvanised her to do something about it far faster.

- Salary – perhaps you work in an industry with clearly defined salary bands or much lower average salary. If salary is a key driver for you, then instead of whinging about the poor pay and feeling defined by it, you could tackle an alternative. Either work out how to change, beat or overcome the salary bands in your organisation, or change industries to somewhere that salary banding or low salaries are not the norm.

- Progress – maybe you've outgrown your role but love the company you work for. Instead of simply remaining static and not doing anything, or resigning and going to an organisation you're uncertain of – talk to your boss or HR about restructuring your role so you can add more value, stay engaged and remain with the organisation you love.

- Opportunity – what would happen if your boss taps you on the shoulder and offers you a new opportunity that you 'don't prefer'? Instead of worrying that this is the only option that will come up and if you say no, then there won't be another option, use it as an opportunity to open up discussions to talk more about other options for increased engagement or adding value in ways you do prefer.

- Parental leave is an interesting one. Many people head into it with the assumption that they will come out worse off afterwards. Unfortunately, here in Australia war stories of poorly handled parental leave are still common. Instead, why not rewrite this narrative for yourself? See it as an opportunity to reshape your role in a way that benefits both you and your organisation.

If you head into your discussions and negotiations scared of failing, then you probably will. But if you head into these discussions with clear intentions, with the benefits clearly outlined for both you and the organisation, then something better may emerge for you. But you need to remain on the front foot and take charge of the narrative.

As Tony Morrison from the Beloved said

"Definitions belong to the definers, not the defined."

The moral of this chapter is to stop letting other people's limitations and beliefs define you. Stop letting your own limitations get in the way. Instead see limitations as the challenge they are - opportunities for growth and development. You are the protagonist in your own story. You decide, then either create the narrative, or rewrite the new narrative if it's not working for you in its current form.

Chapter 7

The Game Plan

Step Up
Speak Out
Take Charge

Chapter 7

The Game Plan

> *"I was not rescued by a prince; I was the administrator of my own rescue."* – Elizabeth Gilbert

The title of this chapter has been chosen deliberately, to imply playfulness and a light touch. I suspect that there are times when we need to take our career seriously, and times when we don't. There are times too when we are taking it seriously, when perhaps a light touch would be better suited and vice versa. Finding the right and appropriate mix for you is important on your sense of achievement, well-being and ability to deliver results for your stakeholders.

Many of us imagine that success is linear with an upward trajectory yet it's more like a game of Snakes and Ladders. In keeping with the metaphor, there will be times when you have a win and can climb a metaphorical ladder. There will be other times when something goes wrong and you slide down a notch or two on a snake. In the moment those situations are intense and dramatic, but we are playing a long game here, so hang in there.

Moving from my career happens to me, to I create my own career

You need to create your own reality. You choose. You need to decide how you'll turn up every day and how you'll respond in any given situation. You need to accept responsibility for making it happen. Open your own doors, step into your own authority and yes; your success starts with you.

You need to acknowledge your own part in all the things that have gone wrong with your career in the past – missed opportunities, project failures, bad bosses, poorly behaved staff, difficult peers – right through to all the things that could potentially go wrong in the future. You also need to own and be able to articulate your part in all the good parts as well; the wins, achievements and successes. Then get out of your own way.

What does this look like in practical terms?

We've all heard stories of amazing women who've found themselves in dire circumstances, somehow manage to pull themselves up by the boot straps, work two jobs, bring up a couple of kids as a single parent and in their spare time create a start-up that goes global.

Some of the highest achieving women I know are busier than most people could begin to imagine. One in particular works full time, has children, volunteers on various Boards and committees, plus studies for an MBA. In general high achievers are great at prioritising and perfect isn't one of their priorities – but getting stuff done and achieving big goals are. Don't forget, every day, *you* get to decide how you spend your time and your energy – and they are the two things that are difficult to get back. Decide wisely.

Choose things that sustain, not drain, things that help you grow, not slow you down.

Ask yourself:

- Do I really need to be watching reruns of *Desperate Housewives*? Or am I merely marking time, waiting for that next big thing to come along and pick me?

- Do I really need to watch two versions of the news on television every night? Or perhaps instead I could be updating my LinkedIn profile or meeting with my new consultant friends who help me see that things could be different.

- Do I really need to sacrifice my goals and dreams for my family all the time, or will they be far better off if I'm re-energised, more engaged in my work life and happier with myself as a person? As women in the workforce we frequently put our needs, desires and wants second, so this can be challenging. Perhaps you're biding your time waiting for kids to leave school, your partner's fast track career or business idea to come to fruition, or perhaps family obligations. It should be like the inflight safety briefing – *"Put your own mask on before helping others."*

In recent years I've come across three instances of highly successful women creating their own new reality. Not only were they also successful in achieving their goals but the strategies were realistic, practical and provide us with new ways of solving old problems. Each of them challenged my own beliefs about what was probable and what was appropriate. Yet each of these ideas excited me about what was possible. In fact, these examples were part of a critical turning point in my own thinking – that taking an active and participatory role in creating your own success is not boasting – it is not only desirable but mandatory for anyone with an iota of ambition.

- Example 1: I met a Life Coach and she had been integral in winning one of her clients the Telstra Business Woman of the Year Award. You guessed it. This super smart client in the wellness sector wasn't leaving things up to chance but decided to tackle the rather daunting process with a coach who focused on confidence, accountability and the language of the business world to keep her in the running and make the effort worthwhile.

- Example 2: Some years back a peer was appointed in a marketing capacity for an organisation – and her main responsibilities for the year were to … (wait for it) … help the female CEO win the Telstra Business Woman of the Year Award. Once again, this smart and strategic CEO acknowledged that her skill set lay in running a company, not winning awards or objectively talking about her own great work. Therefore, she employed someone to tackle the task on her behalf.

- Example 3: I met an author in the final stages of publishing her first book. Her strategy included forsaking her speaker fee at several rather large conferences in return for the organisation who had booked her to speak, purchasing books for all delegates – as presales. And the purpose? To help this smart and strategic new author reach #1 on the New York Times Best Seller list more easily.

If you're feeling stuck or frustrated in your role it's time to let go of being passive and instead make a decision to do things differently. The only person you can change is yourself. So start changing that person now, with a decision. You decide. Step up, or step off.

Learn the Rules of the Career Game

Most of our work environments are still heavily masculinised with masculine models of operating and leading still perceived as better. Until the numbers of women and men who embrace more feminised work practices and leadership styles reach a critical tipping point, this isn't going to change. So learn the rules of this game so you can play the game more effectively and sustainably. Masculine leadership definitely has its place and has stood us in great stead for many years so there is no need to reject it outright. Learn both the obvious rules plus the unwritten ground rules.

Once you've learned the rules then spend time learning how to break them and to work around them as and if required. There is no need for you to embrace the old 80s mantra of "big hair, big shoulder pads, go hard or go home". In fact this will be detrimental to both you and the men and women who follow you. After all, we'll create change far faster and glass ceilings will be a thing of the past, when more women in leadership roles are employing a balance between both the feminine and masculine.

Work On Your Career Not Simply in It

As with great leadership and working on a business, not in it, you'll be rewarded far more and get to where you want to go much faster if you spend time working on your career, not simply in it. This means separating your work from your career management and understanding they are two different things.

It also means spending time setting career goals, creating career plans and executing them.

If you don't know where you are going, how will you know when you get there? Be clear about what you want, where you want to be and by when. Who would you like to work for? Which CEOs or brands/sectors inspire you? Layer over this how much you want to be remunerated. Then spend time reflecting on what it will look and feel like when you get there, otherwise you may miss the moment when it happens.

You probably work in a strategic capacity within the organisation you work for, so do the same for your own career.

Once you define what you are looking for (and a general 'right for right now' goal is okay), allocate at least one action each week on moving the dial on your aspirations. That could be documenting and quantifying wins and achievements for your CV, reaching out to build your networks both inside and outside the business, boosting your skills in areas where you've identified gaps as you head toward your goal, keeping an ideal role scrap book and updating it on a regular basis, taking a course or reading a book that will further your future career prospects, or contributing to discussions on LinkedIn in your area of expertise – to name a few.

Perhaps you're in a career that was dictated by your undergraduate degree ten years ago. Or perhaps you landed a role back when the economic climate was less favourable and it became comfortable over time. Since then you've realised it doesn't actually fire you up and you've been yearning for work that was meaningful. Time to start working on your career again.

Pitching to Win

Instead of giving things a try, or even giving things your best shot – why not pitch to win? We've learned that some women shy away from competition, however many don't. When you treat your career as more of a game with some wins and some losses, some snakes and some ladders, then pitching to win comes more easily. Instead of looking at a role and saying "I can do most but that one bullet point doesn't suit me", tackle it with a more curious approach of "if I were to win this role, what would I need to demonstrate and where else might I find evidence?" Flick the switch from under-estimating, to pitching to win; from proving your worth, to knowing your worth; and from *leaning out* because you aren't likely to win, to having conviction in your abilities to make a difference and going for it anyway.

Learn the Language of Value

When some women describe their professional performance they use language such as "loyal", "hard working", "thorough" and "diligent" – even at a senior professional level. If you can't communicate in language that the C-suite understands; about the problems you solve, the difference you make and the results you deliver - then you'll be bypassed. This means thinking in terms of big picture and context and helping other people to see that what you do contributes to the strategic initiatives of the organisation or longer term goals of your division. It also requires providing evidence and quantifying achievements. Make a weekly habit of quantifying your achievements, so that when you do go to update your

CV or LinkedIn profile, or if you're asked why you're the right person for the role, you've got those demonstrable measurable outcomes clearly articulated. The six monthly CV update is then a far less daunting task because you've been measuring and quantifying regularly.

Fill in the Gaps

"With the right leadership skills, the highest levels of career success are well within reach. Unfortunately, conventional wisdom about leadership won't get you to the top. Much of it is outdated, incomplete, and ineffective. What you need is.........The Missing 33%!"

– Susan Colantuono

Susan Colantuono, a career coach for women based out of the USA, talks about the critical 'missing 33%' in female business education:

- Strategic acumen,

- Financial acumen and

- Business acumen.

Because many women work their way through the ranks in areas such as customer care, human resources, child care, social services and health care, these substantive business acumens are missed. You will be more difficult to overlook in a recruitment process if you fill in these gaps. Don't wait passively to be taught these things. Teach it to yourself. Find people in your current business who can help you with this. Volunteer for projects or on committees, that will give you exposure to those areas of a business. Work with your manager to make sure any substantive gaps in your business education are filled. Make it a priority.

Ensure You Remain Visible

Because the traditional notion of the idealised woman remains as the 'helpmeet' in the background, creating visibility can be challenging for some. Plus we're intuitively navigating a fine line between not talking ourselves up enough and being penalised for talking about ourselves too much. We're far more likely to put our staff forward for an Award than nominate ourselves or suggest a colleague for an opportunity that put our own hand up – and we'd be criticised if we didn't. Or if we do put ourselves forward, we feel guilty, awkward or embarrassed.

Waiting to be noticed is no longer an option. Ensuring you have visibility both inside and outside your organisation is important. No more hiding your light under a bushel. Remember too that everyone is the protagonist in their own movie, so you need to draw attention to yourself, your work and your potential in strategic ways or you'll be bypassed.

Here are some ideas to throw into your mix:

- Establish a LinkedIn strategy that keeps you 'top of the pops' 24/7 with minimal effort by you – activities include connecting with industry peers and leaders, liking articles that others share, sharing or publishing articles around your expertise or personal brand and commenting thoughtfully in group discussions

- Do the same on your intranet at work – make sure that you gain visibility within the business for contributing new ideas, sharing case studies, delivering excellence, aligning with core values, strategic initiatives and vision. If you do attend work conference then summarise findings and learnings and share strategically within the department or business more broadly. Don't wait to be asked. Just do it.

- Actively participate in your peak body or association – volunteer on a committee, offer to assist on seminar programming, emceeing and chairing as a starting point. Choose activities that help you grow your public profile and provide broad recognition, not just working diligently in the background.

- Volunteer to participate in panel discussions

- Volunteer on a special project working party in your organisation

- Be profiled in an industry publication

- Nominate (or be nominated) for an Industry Award (or two) – yes you

- Nominate to be on your industry association Board

- Take an active role in a working group updating your industry Standard or benchmarks

- Speak at an industry conference and then 'shop' the talk around so you get to speak at more than one on the same topic and be known as an expert

- Make sure your peak body/association or industry publication knows that you are happy to be consulted, and quoted, for expert opinion

- Discuss with your communications team your desire to publish on LinkedIn or your own blog and ask for assistance

- Establish a regular and strategic publishing schedule on LinkedIn to start positioning yourself as someone with expertise

- Establish an industry network to support and motivate your own career objectives and invite expert speakers to inspire - consider face to face networking or maybe a discussion group on Facebook or equivalent.

Execute a Bold Hairy Audacious Move Every Now and Then

Every now and then simply get out of your own way, ignore the small voice of the *itty bitty shitty committee* inside your mind, and simply try something that the sensible you would normally dismiss. Execute a big, bold, hairy and audacious move. Give it your best shot but remember this is a game. So do this with a light touch.

- Apply for an opportunity or role where it's a long shot for you to get it, but if you did it would be an amazing opportunity.

- Why not actively and strategically manoeuvre for the opportunity to interview or spend a day with the biggest name in your business?

- Why not apply for a secondment to work with a brand name that really lights your fire?

The best bit with bold audacious moves is that if and when you land them, you will feel like you won the lottery. Ask yourself:

- What have you got to lose if you do? Or perhaps more importantly …

- What have you got to lose if you don't?

It's Not Too Late to Find What it is You Want to be When You Grow Up

While there will be a part of you not wanting to throw the baby out with the bathwater, it's highly likely you've either fallen into your current career without much choice or proactive effort on your part, or you've simply changed. Never fear! It's not too late to spend time working out what you want to be when you grow up.

I know men and women in their 50s who still feel as though they are living a life belonging to someone else. On the flipside I also know of women who have changed career in their later years and gone on to far greater happiness and success as a result. At the end of this chapter are four activities that I suggest you use to explore your options.

In the meantime here are a couple of examples to inspire you

Case study 1:

I know a woman on the motivational speaker circuit. She completed the happiness lifeline many years ago while extricating herself out of a career in finance and accounting. The times when she was happiest were when she was in front of people performing, and this was a common theme throughout her childhood, teenage years and young adulthood. Spring forward 25 years later and, in the middle of a career crisis, she worked out that in order to be really fulfilled she wanted to help people create change in their lives and do that by speaking from the stage. She now flies around the country delivering motivational talks and speeches each month and running personal development retreats in Bali. What a life! What a career! And she created this.

Case study 2:

Another woman I know, and let's call her Mary, has allergies and sensitivities to various foods. The irony is that she is actually a bit of a foodie – loves cooking, loves great food and the good times associated with that. Unfortunately, her allergies, sensitivities and subsequent health impacts have also made it challenging for her to maintain a regular career working 9 – 5 for someone else. She was finding that as part of looking after herself she was spending an inordinate amount of time reading, researching and testing recipes etc., so that she didn't feel like she was missing out on food choices all the time. She is also a very visual person and has always shared pictures of food and amazing dishes on Facebook – many of which seemed to attract that mystical property of going viral.

After some time reflecting and exploring she started a catering business specialising in catering for those with food sensitivities. The benefit is that she is able to dictate her own working hours based on her health, wellness and clients in the pipeline. She is in charge of how much work she accepts or rejects because she is the boss. She gets to play in Facebook groups and provide people with recipes and help others when they reach out. Plus, her business is growing rapidly as more and more people acknowledge they have food sensitivities and would be better off avoiding certain types of food.

Remember this is the career game, and it's your career. You don't need to do anything you don't want to do. Do play boldly and confidently, do treat it with a light touch like you would any other game, and do play a proactive game rather than a defensive game. I can guarantee you'll love the end result far more.

Optional

Exercise 4: What's Important to you About Work Version 2

Step 1: What's important to you about work? We talked about this already as an activity on page 36. Why not do it again but this time instead of focusing on things such as remuneration, flexibility and logistics etc., focus on the content of your work. Modify the question to 'what's important to you about the content of your work'? Allow the answers to free flow. Don't try to rationalise, justify or create stories about why or why not. Accept your responses as they emerge. Aim to fill an A4 page with bullet points. Examples may include – I get to work with people, I have work that makes a difference to other people, I get to grow a business, I get to turn around an organisation.

Step 2: Cull: Start culling your responses down. Pick the top 8.

Step 3: Distil: Reflect on your top 8 and then start eliminating again right down to your one or two main areas.

Exercise 5: If Money Were No Option

Journal – if money were no option, what would you be doing? Take time to reflect, brainstorm and come up with a bunch of ideas. Remember, there is a heap of research that demonstrates that being bored is equally if not more stressful for you than having too much to do. If you decide you want to lay around poolside in Bali, go a little deeper and work out what is it that that lifestyle represents to you. Is it the warm climate that you want? Is it the variety of cultural diversity? Is it that you want to feel like you live in luxury? Is it that you are craving financial security and poolside holidays to Bali are reflective of that? Start to explore and dig deeper than the obvious. See if anything comes to light.

Exercise 6: Happiness Lifeline

Journal –Take a trip down memory lane. Ask yourself when were you most happy. Start at childhood and create a time line as you work your way down your page noting significant moments and specifically when you were most happy, engaged and fulfilled. Don't worry if these moments weren't at work. In fact, I'd be surprised if they were, but do start noticing any common themes. These common themes may pinpoint really enjoyable activities well suited to your personality type or skill set, that you may have suppressed years ago while looking for a role to pay the bills or to keep your parents happy.

Exercise 7: Why not try the 45 Why process?

There is a great technique that is perfect to use when under pressure at work or to help you identify what it is you really want to be doing. It's called the '45 whys'. Basically – you grab a sheet of A4 (or a computer), find quiet time to reflect and document a long list of whys for the work you are doing or the work you want to do.

Ask yourself:

- Why do I want to continue in (insert your field of work or role)? OR

- Why do I want a role as leader in this industry? OR

- Why do I want to be on the (insert company name) Board? OR

- Why do I bother to get out of bed every morning and go to work? OR

- Why might I try something different?

Start writing.

1. ....

2. ....

3. ....

4. ....

5. .... etc.

Don't stop until you have at least 45 reasons. Dig deep. Don't censor or judge. Physical, spiritual, material, personal or professional – it doesn't matter. Feel free to go beyond 45. Sometimes the best reasons come after the obvious.

This activity is perfect before a meeting where the pressure will be on, a job interview, a presentation or a funding pitch. It's ideal when you are feeling down, under the pump or pressured about work. It's also great if you are feeling reflective and simply want to work out once and for all *what it is you want to be when you grow up.*

Chapter 8

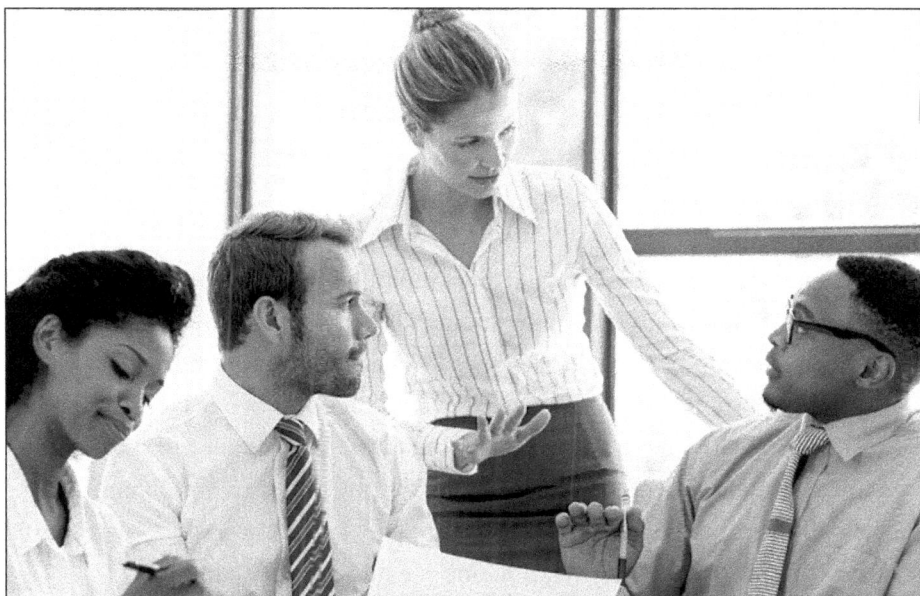

Credibility and Personal Brand Killers

Chapter 8

Credibility and Personal Brand Killers

"And anyway, who wears a tiara on a jungle gym?"

– Sheryl Sandberg

Language Warning!

When it comes to personal brand and credibility there is a piece of the pie that we women need to own. Without wanting to implement a program of 'fixing the women', when it comes to gender politics in the office, like dressing appropriately, we also need to pay attention to our language and speech habits. If we want a seat at the 'big table' then we need to speak like grown-ups and accept responsibility for our own part in a problem. And the following habits that we women frequently demonstrate undermine our credibility and authority all in one – without us even knowing.

Just – the most recent culprit in the language debate is the use of "just". Early in 2015 Ellen Petry Leanse, founder, Karmahacks; strategist, advisor, online pioneer was published in Business Insider calling women out on it.

I was delighted and couldn't agree more, because the word is a pet peeve of mine. I hear this word all the time and mostly from women. Let's be clear, frequently there is no just about it. At the very least the word is redundant – and at the most it diminishes the opinion, status or impact of the request by the initiator/asker.

- "I just wanted to find out…"

- "I was just booking for…"

- "I am just enquiring about…"

- "Just following up…"

- "Just checking in…"

My own research (sample size of about six close personal female friends for brunch) determined that the use of the word is part of our feminine socialisation – not to big note ourselves, not to stand out, not to offend, not to challenge, to be safe and (let's own the negative impact of fashion magazines, dieting and body image too) to be diminutive, small and not a bother.

Do check your emails before you hit send. Listen to your own speech patterns. Then remove 'just'. This one small change makes your communications far more powerful. Try it. You may be surprised at how confident you sound and the results that you get with this one simple change.

Deflecting compliments

Oh girl! And most of us think we are simply doing the right thing.

You know how it goes;

"Oh, it was nothing, it was just *doing my job, in fact the team did most of the work and … the reality is the project didn't go as well as we'd hoped. We hit a few speed bumps in January but we got there in the end…*"

Sound familiar?

It's okay to accept a compliment as it is and simply say thank you. It makes the giver feel good, it boosts your own confidence plus it helps with your own credibility. Repeat after me –

> *"Deflecting compliments undermines credibility.*
> *Accepting compliments boosts it."*

As women we've been taught time and time again not to big note ourselves, not to take credit unless it's totally ours, and not to stand out. Why? Because it's allegedly 'unladylike'.

In a future where women are leading equally with men it's totally unprofessional (non-gender specific) to not accept a compliment. Own it, accept it and dish out a few compliments of your own as you see how they boost the confidence of both the giver and the receiver.

Apologising for strong opinions

> *"Women are 37% more likely than men to identify their own behaviour as worthy of an apology, which leads to women apologising more frequently than men do ... which in turn, unfortunately, fuels the double standard that women who aren't 'apologetic enough' are bossy (or worse)."*
> – Upworthy July 2014

All true and correct according to a 2010 study by Karina Schuman and Michael Ross entitled *Why Women Apologize More Than Men; Gender Differences in Thresholds for Perceiving Offensive Behaviour.*

However, what's more concerning is that as women we sometimes apologise for having strong opinions. You've probably heard it in meetings or in strong discussions where sometimes, if a woman lands a contrary opinion, she apologises.

You've already learned to let go of the need to be right. So now accept responsibility for your own thoughts, ideas and opinions. They are simply that; thoughts, ideas and opinions, not "truths". These thoughts, ideas and opinions are based on the evidence you have access to at that time.

As women we apologise even when it's not our fault – when we bump elbows with someone on the plane next to us, when we are startled and when we talk over someone. Sheryl Sandberg says it's because have been told we are too bossy since we were little girls. Sound familiar?

It's ingrained into us and a hard pattern to break. But if you want to see evidence of what a difference it makes then get online and check out Pantene's powerful 'sorry' campaign – demonstrating the power of turning off your automatic sorry response.

Uptalk

More commonly known as ending a sentence that is not a question with an upward inflection – resulting in it sounding uncertain, or like it could possibly *be* a question. In a 2014 BBC article entitled *The Unstoppable March of The Upward Inflection*, linguistics experts call attention to the rise of the upward inflection and how it sounds like we are asking for permission all the time. This in turn diminishes your power, your credibility and authority.

If you have any ambitions to head up a team, lead an organisation or influence others to join you in your new venture you'll want to knock this one on the head – immediately.

Linguistic experts don't really know where it came from but it's fairly widespread and, unfortunately Australian and New Zealand women are rather expert at it.

Picture this – you are a high performer, a perfectionist, with an eye for your next big promotion. You go in for your performance appraisal and you are extremely well prepared. In outlining your last 12 months work, your achievements and the demonstrable measurable outcomes, every second statement you make ends with an upward inflection – which sounds like a question.

- Where is the power in this conversation?

- How credible do you think it sounds?

More importantly, it sounds like you are seeking permission, rather than making statements or taking charge of the narrative – thereby undermining your best attempts at negotiating that extra pay rise, next big promotion or rock star rating on your appraisal.

What about meeting behaviours?

Meetings are another forum where I've observed women making credibility errors they aren't aware of. Here are my favourites.

Making coffee or note taking

As a woman with a formerly big job title, I have always been careful to aim for equality and balance in the meeting makeup and division of roles and responsibilities. However, my own mentor once pointed out to me that I frequently played the 'hostess game' (a role I was extremely comfortable with) which in the eyes of some diminished my contribution in a meeting before I'd even had the chance to contribute. Anecdotal evidence tells us that women frequently do this. Adam Grant and Sheryl Sandberg, in their New York Times article *Madam CEO, Get Me a Coffee*, articulate clearly how time and time again these behaviours (and expectations) keep women playing small – by diminishing our contribution and our own gravitas. The irony is that if a man does these same house office duties he is showered with praise and positive acknowledgement!

> *"The person taking diligent notes in the meeting almost never makes the killer point."*
>
> – Sheryl Sandberg and Adam Grant

Not getting to the point

As women we are generally known to be, and take pride in being, great communicators. From an evolutionary perspective good communication and using language to make meaning is the glue that holds communities together. But in our time-poor meeting environments, defensively over explaining because we feel like we're coming from a position of lesser power, can sometimes get in the way and hamper clear and effective communications with those of the opposite sex. In short, some women frequently use a lot of words, making references to people and situations not directly relevant to the meeting outcomes, when fewer words could make a bigger difference.

Asking if people understood you

You know when you get to the end of trying to explain something in a meeting and the person opposite you is looking at you like they don't really know what you are talking about? What some women habitually do is then ask "was I clear?" or "do you understand what I mean?"

We're trying to be helpful but there is an assumption in that question that it was your fault that the other person didn't understand. Possibly instead, they are simply playing catch up or instead of listening, they've been working out what they will say next in response.

Don't assume that you weren't the one being clear. If you've practiced all the above steps, then you're being clear and articulate anyway. The very act of asking if they understood you puts the blame and doubt back onto you. It's a habit that you need to break. Learn to break it early before it does your reputation too much damage.

"You wouldn't worry so much about what others think of you if you realized how seldom they do." – Eleanor Roosevelt

---

Being too abrupt or strident

This is something some of us do in our efforts to beat the biology and biases, and not succumb to our socialisation. This behaviour backfires by potentially alienating both men and women. My own personal version included a stance of *suffering no fools* and *taking no prisoners* when presenting arguments with my very direct *get with the program* presentation style. As a result, great projects and plans were put on a go-slow. Counterproductive to say the least!

Yes, there is unconscious bias at play, whereby men and women will judge women negatively and see her as bossy (even if she's not), when she is being strong and direct. And until the bias in these situations is eliminated, we need to find a way to work around it.

What can you do about it?

The ego's deep, ingrained need for approval is hard to fix – so you'll need to be vigilant.

- Next time you have a conversation, I challenge you to record yourself and listen for the tone and melody of your conversation. Listen out also for apologies, the word 'just', and demurring when complimented. Determine whether or not they were necessary – or simply ingrained patterning, people pleasing or seeking approval behaviours.

- Ask a trusted colleague, coach or mentor to give you feedback next time you are in a meeting or in a situation where you feel stressed or uncertain. Ask them to identify and note specifically any verbal tics that are getting in the way of clear communication and your leadership aspirations.

- Rehearse a few times and then record yourself again and listen for what's really going on. 'Fake it till you make it' is probably great advice in this instance.

- I've even heard of a manager using these notes on language and meeting behaviours as teaching points with her entire team (men and women) to ensure the department operated more efficiently and effectively – supporting each other and getting better outcomes for the division as a result The department was frequently the meat in the sandwich when it came to providing feedback to the business about customer sentiment. Providing feedback works better when it comes from a place of credibility rather than uncertainty.

- There are also software plugins that you can insert into your email software that act like spellcheck but instead look out for credibility killers such as 'just', 'sorry', 'actually' or 'I'm no expert but...'. Worth the investment in my book.

- If you must play hostess, find a gracious way to involve both men and women in the housekeeping tasks (i.e. rotating responsibilities). Alternatively, allocate staff not involved in the content of the meeting to take on those responsibilities. If someone asks you to get them a coffee and you don't believe that is your role at the time, politely decline and suggest that you too would like someone to bring a coffee.

- Learn to get to the point quickly, succinctly and clearly. Say it once, clearly and articulately. Let it land. That's it. No need to repeat it. Practice and rehearse with a trusted colleague or mentor outside of the meetings structure.

- A highly successful consultant I know suggests that as women we would be well served to learn to frame a verbal report with "I'll speak to the result first, and then if required I can provide the detail and process". This frame enables you to get to the point quickly then provide context and meaning if required.

- Don't assume that you are the person not explaining well. If you've been implementing my suggestions all along, you will have been rehearsing and refining your skills anyway.

- Find the mid-ground, the balance between waffling on too long or being too abrupt and strident. Once again, practice out loud with a trusted colleague or mentor – focus on memorable sound bites (gleaned from media or comms training), story-telling techniques that have been proven to work and also varying both tone and pitch.

Why are these things important?

We're in interesting times right now. As women we want to lead but frequently find the journey there is not easy at the best of times, and downright challenging at the worst. You want to make sure that your 'feminine ambition tool kit' is fitted out with the best of the best, sharpest, high quality tools that help you get ahead more easily. Credibility, authority and expertise are great tools – and we need to make sure that we don't accidentally undermine ourselves despite best efforts and intentions.

Chapter 9

15 Negotiation Tips and Traps to Help You Get Ahead

Chapter 9:

15 Negotiation Tips and Traps to Help You Get Ahead

At one period in my first year of mentoring and coaching nearly every single one of my clients asked for advice on salary negotiation – and the irony is that many of them were negotiation experts in and of their own right.

This got me thinking. Why is it that these women don't like negotiating? It can't be that they aren't good at it because these particular women are highly sought after dispute resolution experts and do really well advocating for others. What else is going on?

- Is it because there is a social stigma attached to negotiating on your own behalf?

- Is it because women are perceived as greedy if and when we do, and greed is associated with appetite?

Possibly and probably. Anyone who is anyone knows that appetite and women are two words that don't go together comfortably in a sentence even in this day and age. But when we are going after big career or entrepreneurial goals our appetites will show whether we like it or not. If we want something hard enough it's difficult to hide! And neither we should. Ambition is not a dirty word despite what some would have us believe.

Here are fifteen interesting findings for women, perception and negotiation that will simply blow your mind or at least help you navigate the likeability divide far more easily.

1. Take ownership of our part in the problem

We need to take ownership of the fact that we avoid negotiating for ourselves.

As you've already read, according to Linda Babcock, a professor of economics at Carnegie Mellon University and the author of *Women Don't Ask,* men negotiate four times more frequently than women, and women ask for 30% less when we do ask.

I've personally spoken with many an HR manager and recruiter. They agree that women ask for raises less frequently and also ask for less when they do. We need to own this piece of the puzzle when reflecting on getting ahead – and be prepared to do something about it. Leadership requires you to stand out from the crowd. Not being a statistic is the first step.

2. It's easier and more beneficial to have someone else do your negotiation for you

Hannah Riley Bowles, a Senior Lecturer in Public Policy at the Harvard Kennedy School and Research Director of its Women and Public Policy Program, says that "Women do substantially better negotiating for others than for themselves" and that "It's got to do with social stereotypes".

According to Bowles, when we as women negotiate hard for ourselves, there is a social cost, as we come out looking less likeable. And once again we're back to navigating that double edged sword between 'nice girl' and 'hard-nosed b*tch'.

And while it's not always possible to have a salary broker advocating on your behalf, it's possible we need to accept the social cost in the short term, because the very real cost in dollars is undermining us later in life. Over the course of a career maybe a short term drop in perceived likeability is a small price to pay?

The first step is to ensure that in your own department there is no disparity, and do your best to influence policies, procedures and mechanisms in your organisation that ensure that gender salary gap isn't systemic. Then get to work ensuring you aren't undermining yourself.

3. **Stop talking up how well you do the job – and start talking up the value you add**

As you've already read, as women we frequently get stuck in the mode of doing the job properly and well, as if 'doing the job well' were the end result. But when something new comes along or we start dreaming of something better, all we have is the language and experience of 'doing the job well'.

Carrie Gallant, negotiation expert from Canada, talks about leveraging value. Be sure to bring the value of what you offer to the table – context and big picture thinking – and communicate that clearly and articulately.

> *"Leverage is essentially what you bring that is valuable to someone else, plus your ability to help them see that value ... "*
> – Carrie Gallant

Start identifying the links between what you do and the organisation's strategic agenda. Look for how your work contributes to things like profitability, productivity, better governance and risk, increased customer satisfaction or staff engagement to name a few. Find the evidence and quantify it.

Do this every week as a routine. Here's their formula for collecting evidence and reinforcing positive learnings about achievements. Identify:

- What the achievement was

- The benefit you delivered (financial or otherwise)

- The core skill used to deliver that achievement

Imagine how useful it would be to have done this well in advance of a performance appraisal, salary re-negotiation or even in preparation for your quarterly CV or LinkedIn profile update. Imagine too how well prepared you'll feel the next time someone challenges you in a meeting or questions your output.

4. Three feminine super powers that are great for negotiating

Tara Mohr, of *Playing Big*, writes about a really interesting study where men and women were paired in mock negotiation. Some of the pairs of negotiators were told that traits frequently associated with women were great for negotiation:

- Active listening,

- Emotional intelligence, and

- Good communication skills

Guess what! In the pairs who were given this information the women outperformed the men. Additionally these three skills or characteristics are usually categorised as 'feminine'.

So, instead of heading into a negotiation worrying that you aren't good at it, focus instead on the skills that you do have (listening, emotional intelligence and communication) and leverage those for more beneficial outcomes.

5. Don't think of yourself as a woman negotiating (beat the stereotype effect)

I'm extrapolating here – but the following research may throw some light on this point. In 1999 Margaret Shih conducted a study at Harvard University of 46 undergraduate Asian women. They were asked to sit a maths test (with maths traditionally thought of as a masculine strength). When the women were reminded of their femininity prior to the test, their test scores dropped compared to a control group. Interestingly when the Asian women were reminded of their Asian heritage (with the stereotype excelling at math) they didn't perform anywhere near as poorly.

How can we use this? When heading into a negotiation, which is stereotypically seen as the domain of the masculine, be sure to do so with a growth mindset and well clear of your usual stereotypically feminine activities. Once again, remind yourself of examples of where you've performed well before in negotiating great outcomes, instead of remembering examples of where you've not done so well.

7. Reframe your language from 'negotiating' to 'asking' and you'll more likely ask for a raise

Apparently the word 'negotiation' has negative connotations for many women. In a study entitled *Who goes to the bargaining table? The influence of gender and framing on the initiation of negotiation,* published in 2007 by the American Psychological Association, demonstrates that by using language such as 'asking' which is perceived as less intimidating, more polite and more role consistent, women are more likely to initiate negotiations.

"Consequently, gender differences in initiating negotiations persisted when situations were framed as opportunities for negotiation yet were eliminated when situations were framed as opportunities to ask."

– Deborah A Small, Michele Gelfand, Linda Babcock and Hillary Gettman

Ah the power of language to reframe. Ask, don't negotiate – even though the connotation of permission seeking doesn't sit well with me, we need to remember our *why* – and if asking makes you more likely to negotiate a raise, then ask away.

8. You are not likely to be any more or any less successful than men

In a recent *Harvard Business Review* article, Margaret A. Neale and Thomas Z Lys write that "When both men and women have similar expectations about compensation packages, there is no difference in their likelihood to negotiate. Empirical evidence also shows that when women do negotiate, they're no more or less successful than their male counterparts."

Remember and be encouraged by this. As a woman you are not likely to be any more or any less successful than your male counterparts when asking for a raise. Stop hesitating because you *know it will never work*, or *think it's not worth it* and do go ahead and ask. The evidence on the gender salary gap is clear. We know that on average men are paid more for doing the same work. We also know they ask more frequently than women. We now also know that they are not likely to be any more successful in the negotiation than us when they do ask. Do go ahead and ask. You may be successful.

9. Lift your game

> *"Work out what you'd like, double it, then add 20%. That's your asking price."*

I use this formula as a fun discussion starting point with audiences to gauge a reaction about what motivates them, limitations vs challenges mindset and their current perception of their own value and worth. What's sad is that the men in the room nearly always have a far higher starting point than the women and absolutely always have a higher end asking price. We've talked about bias, socialisation and the system that gets in the way, but I suspect we women also could do with lifting our own game. We're going to tackle our professional career very differently if we're aiming for $100k per annum compared with if we're aiming for $400K per annum. We'll make different choices, we'll make a very different plan and we'll look for opportunities that are remunerated differently.

10. Reframe the conversation to collaborative problem solving

Reframe your negotiation (or asking) from a fight or justification conversation to a collaboration and problem solving activity. You are helping your manager solve the problem of remunerating you as you would like, plus meet organisational objectives! When we do this the negotiation becomes more of a win–win. It's really hard to think that someone is 'hard-nosed' and 'greedy' when you are helping them solve their problems.

11. It's not all about the dollars

In speaking with recruiters, they tell me that sometimes people get hung up on the *big number* when they might be better off emotionally and/or financially with asking for flexibility in working from home, starting/finishing late, extra leave, or additional training, mentoring or coaching included in their package. Flexibility around your thinking about these things can be more rewarding for both men and women all around.

I'm not advocating that women accept less money than men for performing the same role. Quite the reverse. Instead I'm advocating an honest analysis of your current situation. It may be worth more to you to ask your employer for other solutions instead.

12. Do your research and align yourself with others

Find out what industry benchmarks and standards there are, how you compare, what else is going on in industry and other case studies where things have been successful. According to Sheryl Sandberg of *Lean In* fame – if you refer to other perspectives it lends legitimacy to your argument and demonstrates that you've thought this through. When you refer to 'we' it again adds credibility – you are part of a bigger picture.

13. The Sheryl Sandberg effect

Yes, there is such a thing as a 'Sheryl Sandberg effect'. Apparently after the release of *Lean In*, women were hitting up their boss for raises with lines such as: "Sheryl Sandberg would be disappointed in me if I didn't ask for a raise". The reference suggests that you've done your homework, you're taking your career seriously as well as aligning yourself to a cause (the success of women everywhere). It certainty can't hurt.

14. Do it all at once

When you do negotiate (or renegotiate) do so all at once, not in dribs and drabs throughout the year. Sounds counterintuitive, doesn't it?

But when you are asking for things throughout the year you are trying to 'win each battle' one issue at a time. When you negotiate a package all at once you are more likely to be able to come to a solution that meets the needs of both parties.

15. Do your preparation

Work out what your non-negotiable items are, then document a range of scenarios in case they say *yes* to this item but *no* to that item. How might you respond? How might you counter? How might they respond? Use a negotiation preparation sheet like the one on my website www.AmandaBlesing.com. Use it to work out what's negotiable, what's non-negotiable, what are your priorities, where might you be prepared to be flexible, and flexible in return for what?

Remember, you want to go into a negotiation feeling buoyant and confident enabling you to flick the switch:

- From feeling defensive to feeling self-assured

- From feeling like you need to prove your worth, to knowing your worth

- From feeling like you need to convince people that you know what you're valuable, to having conviction about the difference you make, the problems you solve and the value you add.

Dan Pink, in his book *To Sell Is Human*, uses the term 'buoyancy' and talks about how important it is to remain optimistic and agile in a sales environment. Well, negotiating for yourself is in part a sales environment – you are influencing others to your way of thinking and selling the value of what you deliver. We can learn from this as we approach as we form our plan. As Pink puts it:

"Ask yourself questions beforehand ('Can I succeed?') rather than pumping yourself up ('I am the best'); these questions encourage your mind to come up with answers, reasons, and intrinsic motivation."

Don't forget to embrace the growth mindset too. Remember the three provisos from Chapter 6?

- You need to be prepared to make mistakes,

- You need to be prepared to be uncomfortable

- You need to be prepared to do the work.

I'd like to add one more proviso – *hope is not a strategy*. It's not like doing a bungee jump and closing your eyes before you jump. Do the preparation, make a plan and execute.

When it comes to tackling salary package negotiations for ourselves, which many people find uncomfortable, it's best to do it with an understanding that you'll simply keep on getting better at it the more you do it.

And finally – while it never feels like a good time to have a tough conversation, but part and parcel of leadership is learning to do exactly that.

The right time, while not perfect, is now.

It's your career and your future – and your ability to navigate, and negotiate, that double-edged sword between *nice girl and hard-nosed b*tch*, will be in part what helps you be more successful in what ever direction your career takes you.

Chapter 10

Leverage your Expertise, Network and Experience

Chapter 10:

Leverage your Expertise, Network and Experience

Leverage is one of those marketing terms that most of us don't really understand or fully utilise but it is a tool that's definitely available for us to take advantage of. In fact, that is probably the best definition – to take advantage of something, or use something to maximum advantage. You read earlier that Carrie Gallant talks about your being able to leverage what others think is valuable as a bargaining chip, but you can leverage things for yourself.

1. Leverage your Expertise

As you move further towards your leadership goals, you want to move from trading time for money to trading your expertise for money. By the time most people have been in the workforce for 10+ years we've developed many different expertise that we can leverage.

There is, for example, the direct application of your expertise, or there is the leveraged opportunity provided by your expertise. Most of us get focused on the direct application and definition of our skillset that we don't easily see other options.

If you work in event management then you can apply your event management skills/expertise directly to running events, and then repeatedly run more events... or you could find other ways you can apply this expertise by: running/convening higher level meetings, hosting retreats, writing articles about running events, teaching others in your organisation how to run events, using events management as a metaphor for teaching business principles, creating an app for event managers, publishing a magazine or blog site about common mistakes in event management (#eventfail), volunteering at your kid's school or a charity to professionalise their events management, teaching at an educational institution in events management, or travelling overseas to see how others run events. You could even transition into project management (with the right training), because event management and project management have much in common. You name it, you can probably do it. All of a sudden your events management expertise provides far more opportunities for you.

Why? Because those leveraged opportunities position you as an expert, with wisdom and experience. And those with expertise, along with the benefit of wisdom and experience are more likely to be able to leverage raises, promotions and opportunities.

How else can you use your current set of skills and expertise? How else could they be leveraged?

2. Leverage your Network

Examine your existing network and see who is potentially of value to helping you with your next career move. Can they help with door opening, accountability, confidence boosting, honest feedback, technical expertise, problem solving, introductions or all of the above?

If you're at all like me and brought up with a fiercely independent blueprint then you've probably imagined you need to get ahead all on your own. However success doesn't work that way. Frequently getting ahead requires time, energy, strategy – and support from your network.

I recommend an offer of reciprocity. While people love to help and to feel needed, it's wise to not be the person who only gets in contact when they have something to sell or want something. Once you've identified those in your network who might be beneficial to your future career plans, why not send articles of interest or offer to assist in some way, in addition to asking for assistance yourself?

If you are going in to ask for people's assistance straight off, I highly recommend the "can I buy you a cup of coffee?" type approach. People know what to expect with a coffee meeting:

- It takes approximately 30 mins so is achievable for most, and not too long in case you don't really get on

- It can be at a location convenient to them

- It's inexpensive so no-one feels obligated

- It's casual – so there are no formalities to observe other than basic good manners and professional courtesy

- And if a coffee meeting is not something the person wants to do, it's casual enough for them to decline without damaging the relationship.

A subset of leveraging your network is in creating a strategic network to support you throughout your career.

a) Create a mini mastermind circle of three career or business minded and ambitious friends. You'll want at least three friends in your ambitious mastermind circle – friends (male or female) who support you to stretch in your career, who allow you a safe environment to brag, discuss learning opportunities, talk about management or leadership and discuss strategy.

Courtesy of spending hours upon hours in the foyer of five star hotels in capital cities around Australia, one of the things I notice that men and women do differently is the way that they network, even in informal settings. When women meet each other in these foyers they do so with polite greetings about health and family, followed closely by compliments on appearance or outfit. There may be some fleeting or passing reference to work, but it's never really dwelled upon unless something is going wrong – in which case the issue is explored, examined and dissected in great detail.

While there is nothing wrong with this, the conversations I observe between male peers are very different beasts. These masculine conversations have a different energy, rhythm and focus. The conversation is nearly all about work, career and achievement, with a few comments dedicated to conversation about wellbeing and family. It frequently focuses on goals, plans and strategies that worked, didn't work, or are in the pipeline.

While I'm sure there is a downside to this masculine conversation, there is definitely an upside. When women don't discuss career strategy, we are missing out on those opportunities to rehearse strategic discussions in a safe setting. These are invaluable moments in which we can rehearse the cut and thrust of adversarial discussion; pitch an idea and hear how it lands; talk up our wins; and relish mistakes as the learning opportunities they are, without agonising over what went wrong.

Women need to step outside their supportive conversational comfort zone and find others who relish talking about boardroom debates, who enjoy discussing attempts to influence the CEO or pitch to the CFO for funding, or who want to discuss BHAGs for five years down the track, with no fear of judgment if those goals are never achieved.

I suspect that our perfectionist tendencies keep us from putting those BHAGs in the open, in case a friend will judge negatively. Yet the very nature of friendship should be supportive. It doesn't matter if we put a goal out there and it doesn't come off to plan. What does matter is when we don't even try.

In my own circle of acquaintance, I have three friends who support me in different ways. Yes, we discuss health, wellness and family. Every now and then we even discuss clothing and appearance, but only as a strategic tool towards achieving our career goals.

- With one I discuss boardroom strategy. She is a company secretary and lawyer by training and I love the opportunity to compare notes about the strategic thinking that goes into preparing Board papers; cautionary tales; and financial or governance issues to be aware of – commercial in confidence of course.

- With another, we discuss BHAGs. We mutually test ideas with each other and share opportunities that will help us achieve our goals. It's liberating. There is no obligation for either of us to do what we talk about, unless we want to. There is no shame in not achieving our goals. But it's great to have a friend to try out ideas on.

- My final 'girlfriend' support is someone who enjoys discussing and rehearsing sales techniques. Yep, we rehearse, refine and laugh about sales pitches together – some successful, some not so much.

What's most important is that I enjoy the very real and meaningful conversations I have with these women. They aren't work conversations per se, but they are about career and strategies that work in a professional environment. After all, work and achievement consumes a significant amount of our time and energy, and if you love your job, why would you relegate it to something you only think about between nine and five?

Which of your friends do you gather around you to support you with your ambitious career goals and strategies? How can you find career minded friends who want to have strategic and career oriented conversations with you?

b) Create a network of champions, mentors and sponsors

Once again, use the rule of three:

- Three people who champion you – those in your business or industry who you've met or worked with/for, who like the way you work and would put your name forward when an opportunity should arise, or suggest you take an opportunity when they see it. It is important that these people are well connected, in the right place at the right time, and if possible, are a little entrepreneurial.

- Three people who push you – coaches, mentors and great (former) bosses – people who hold you accountable. These people aren't afraid to give you feedback, nor are you afraid to ask it of them. They can see when you are getting in your own way, when you need a push or you need support. These people have the benefit of perspective. They also know you well enough to call you on your stuff. We've all got stuff (life) going on. I've got it, you've got it, everyone's got it. After all, everything we do is stuff (life). Sometimes stuff feels overwhelming. Sometimes stuff takes over. Sometimes we don't pay enough attention to stuff. And sometimes we can't see the stuff for the trees and need to be called on it. You'll achieve far more, far more easily with those who push you on your team.

c) Connections

Another subset of leveraging your networks is that of leveraging your connections. In this modern world of hyper-connectivity, with information and connections as high value commodities, he or she who has most connections certainly appears to win. And it's never too late to start. It doesn't matter what your career path, whether it be in sales, in business, in strategy, logistics, people focused organisations or ASX-listed companies, well connected people tend to do better. And yes, you can be an introvert and yet still be well connected.

How do you build connections? Don't dismiss the old fashioned networking event – as nothing beats the opportunity to put a face to a name with a real human connection. Networking without meeting is a bit like online dating, where everything you write on your profile is subjective. 'Outgoing' to a marketing professional might be at a different end of the spectrum to 'outgoing' for a software programmer.

However, there are smarter ways to use your time, such as by connecting with someone on social media first and then backing that up with a face to face connection at a networking event, coffee meeting or industry conference.

LinkedIn and Twitter are content-driven social media platforms that can be utilised in a professional setting. Note to women – data indicates that men are stronger users of both. In order to level out the playing field, we need to get over our discomfort or unfamiliarity with these tools and use them to our advantage – leverage them along with the principle of social proof (if other people like them, they must be okay). If you have lots of Twitter followers and a highly credible feed at first glance, you get credit for that. The same goes on LinkedIn. If you have 500+ connections, a well-constructed profile with recommendations and lots of endorsements, you regularly share or like highly professional articles, or you comment credibly in groups or discussions then this goes to improving your professional credibility – which you can leverage in the future.

Think of it this way – if LinkedIn is to Seek, as Uber is to the taxi industry – then it's imperative we start increasing our skills and familiarity with LinkedIn in order to keep in the game.

d) Professional bodies or associations

Many people join peak bodies or associations because it's the professional thing to do, they offer great networking and education, or because it's mandatory for maintaining professional standards. However, most people don't proactively take advantage of their membership with any real intent. Throughout my 20-year career in the association sector, I only ever saw one person thoroughly leverage their membership well and here are some of the things she did.

When she joined, she sent a letter with the membership application which included:

- Why she was joining and how delighted she was

- A request for a meeting with the CEO to learn more about utilising her membership to best advantage and finally,

- A list of a few things she could do in return for the association – such as writing articles, contributing as an expert commentator, sitting on committees, speaking at events or on webinars, assisting us with marketing and helping us with any public relations type support or advice

Of course she was invited to comment, speak, write, volunteer, be on committees and provide support during her time as a member and of course it helped her grow her own network, opportunities and credibility within a very short period of time.

While the approach is overkill for some, because we frequently join an association because we are new to a profession or industry, this proactive approach certainly fast tracked her way into an industry in which she was relatively new.

3. Leverage your Experience

Most of us have a much broader range of experiences than we ever let on at work. Many of the people I know have been through three or four career iterations, changed roles multiple times, plus have other passions and interests on the side that help round them out as a person. But sometimes when moving up the ranks we focus narrowly on the skill set and direct experiences of work when a broader approach would yield better results.

Why not leverage the knowledge and insights from these other experiences in ways that make a difference in your role or your efforts to create a career that counts?

For example, if you've won medals for sporting achievements, drawing upon the insights and wisdom of how you prepared, how you dealt with failure, how you dealt with winning, and how that then applies at work could be a great way to illustrate a point, communicate more clearly, or demonstrate your understanding of personal leadership or of coaching staff.

Example two – if your experience is around raising a well-adjusted and connected family, then take the time to find the parallels that exist with better managing people, and create stories, examples and analogies to illustrate some of the thinking behind your methods. Then use your experience to springboard you in your managerial aspirations.

Example three – I lived overseas for three years in PNG. I certainly wasn't working in my area of choice during that time. In fact, at one point I was made an offer of a role with an aside that went like this, "Let's give the little woman a little something to keep her busy". And while I was horrified at the time, I'm now in a position where I'm leveraging my PNG experiences and learnings frequently in many ways such as:

- Creating a connection and finding common ground with people who also have a PNG connection

- Sharing great exciting stories about risk and reward, different cultures, high adventure and colourful characters that I can use to illustrate my own teachings,

- Drawing upon these experiences when I'm feeling boring or down. I simply drag out some of those experiences I had there and am reminded of how exciting life can be

You name it; you can leverage it.

4. Leverage your reputation – take control of the narrative before it takes control of you

Your reputation is your brand and in this crazy mixed-up world of social media, the internet and intranet, your personal brand and your professional brand are intertwined. In fact, this is so important that you really want to get this right because this transcends job role and company and you can carry your personal brand wherever you go. You can develop your brand by growing your professional reputation in industry by proactively writing, commenting/commentating, sharing, contributing or speaking. You can boost the professional with the personal – how easy you are to get along with, how well you manage people's expectations (upward and downward), your integrity, your values, your willingness to be part of the team, your willingness to solve problems, your keenness to put forward new ideas and your willingness to step up and lead when required.

You can also do the groundwork by harnessing the power of social media in both the personal and the professional settings. You need to leverage your reputation on social media for future potential gains in the credibility bank. Think of it this way – a new employer would be lucky to have you. It's only they don't know about you yet. Go ahead and boost your credibility on these mostly free platforms, in case this becomes the differentiator in you getting ahead. Why not share or comment on articles that are aligned with professionalism or futuristic thinking in your industry? Moving into the future, employers will be looking for people who can think, clearly articulate themselves, develop arguments and are prepared to take a stand. Social media platforms enable you to do this.

LinkedIn is also a platform where you can create a powerful personal advertisement for brand you. Your profile, if structured correctly, is basically your personal advertising platform 24/7. You can be in a meeting, at an offsite, or on leave – and if your profile is structured well, has the right key words in it, is backed up with endorsements and legitimate recommendations, plus you are strategically active in the right way, at the right times, with the right tone – you don't have to do much else. Learn the LinkedIn game before it's too late or you'll miss the boat. And even if a new platform comes along to take over, you will surely be able to leverage all the credit and endorsements in a pre-emptive way as you transition over.

You saw I mentioned recommendations in the section above. By this I mean testimonials from previous colleagues, staff or managers, people who have attended events you've spoken at or provided a service for. Be selective, as you do want credible looking recommendations. On LinkedIn these recommendations are gold. Not only do they improve your rankings but they also provide that oh so important social proof that you are as good as you say you are.

Conclusion

Be Leaderly -
Bring Your Own Chair

Conclusion

Be Leaderly - Bring Your Own Chair

The thing about Stepping Up, Speaking Out and Taking Charge is that you find that you've started your own apprenticeship in personal leadership – and more specifically you've begun to create the type of leadership that you want to embody.

Forget old patriarchal models of top down leadership that you have grown up with as a child, which were based on old models of law enforcement, the military or even religion. Forget also those idealised feminine models of leadership where grace and poise were held up as the only options available to us.

Instead focus on leadership frameworks that resonate for you – personal leadership, people focused leadership, feminine leadership, adaptive leadership and a leadership style that solves problems for business and community. Because people lead people, not things. Because people will be the ones who inherit the future and want to inhabit the future we've created.

Get over the notional fairy-tale ending, happy ever after assumptions, and leaving things to work out in the wash. Work is not a talent quest with a winner taking all – and the idea of *the universe providing* is not be all it's cracked up to be.

In fact, creating your own reality is rewarding all in its own right and has a life cycle all of its own.

- Stepping up into your own authority, taking ownership and making the decision is the first step.

- Speaking out, finding your voice, putting yourself first, asking for what you need and want, embracing your inner expert and sharing your insights to inspire others is the next step.

- Taking charge – creating a new reality for both yourself and others is the final step, with the proviso that you understand this is a continuous loop.

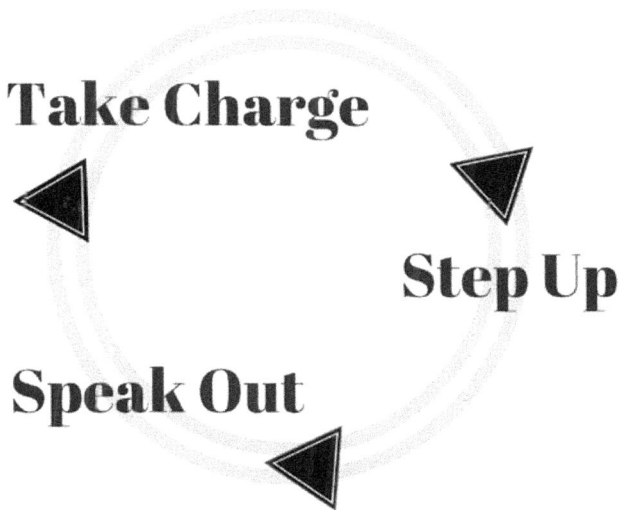

Take Charge

Step Up

Speak Out

The Ambition Revolution

Not only will you find that you are creating a reality and career of your choice far more easily, but instead of waiting for retirement or your golden years to do meaningful work or contribute in significant ways, you'll be making a bigger difference far sooner and far more easily.

We women are resilient, strong, powerful, unique and amazingly talented individuals. While some are born to lead, many create and recreate themselves as leaders at any age. We are eminently capable of running and leading homes, communities, governments and organisations – so why not give it a go? We simply need to see this as an option, then have the courage to think boldly and differently, to challenge the stereotypes and status quo, then Step Up, Speak Out and Take Charge whether others expect us to or not.

Remember – my goal is that you win the feminine ambition trifecta – earn an awesome salary, develop a powerful voice and make an even bigger difference.

Vive la révolution!

#AmbitionRevolution #FeminineAmbition #LookOutCSuiteHereSheComes

About the Author

Approximately 20 years ago Amanda started to work her way through the ranks of association management, with her last role as CEO of SOCAP Australia (the professional association for customer care and complaint professionals). And while she has a strong understanding of how to turn an organisation around, her expertise and passion remains in helping people do better work.

As the creator of The Ambition Revolution program, she currently speaks with, and consults to, busy and ambitious professionals. What really switches her on is seeing these individuals step up, speak out and take charge – of their roles, careers, aspirations and their departments and/or organisations. You might even say Amanda is like a personal trainer for those who are ready to strive for ambitious goals or projects but who need that extra push, strategic focus or confidence boost.

What differentiates her is that despite humble origins in regional South Australia she has big dreams, is determined, self-assured and provides a great example of hands on leadership that navigates the stormy waters between likeability and getting things done. She truly understands and provides solutions for the challenges professionals face in balancing a demanding role, ambition and workload, along with a fulfilling personal life.

Resources

Step Up
Speak Out
Take Charge

Resources

Further reading and websites

www.AmandaBlesing.com

www.AmbitionRevolution.com

https://www.wgea.gov.au – Australian based resource centre for workplace gender equality

Lean In: Women, Work, and the Will to Lead by Sheryl Sandberg
http://leanin.org

The Confidence Code by Katty Kay and Claire Shipman
http://theconfidencecode.com

Mindset: The New Psychology of Success by Carol Dweck
http://mindsetonline.com

Nerve: Poise Under Pressure, Serenity Under Stress, and the Brave New Science of Fear and Cool by Taylor Clark
http://www.taylorclarkbooks.com

Playing Big: Practical Wisdom for Women Who Want to Speak Up, Create and Lead by Tara Sophia Mohr http://www.taramohr.com

Quiet: The Power of Introverts in a World That Can't Stop Talking by Susan Cain http://www.quietrev.com

Think, Decide Act – How to Make Effective Decisions Fast Using Emergency Protocols by Russell Boon www.russellboon.com

Thrive: The Third Metric to Redefining Success and Creating a Happier Life by Arianna Huffington http://ariannahuffington.com/thrive

www.ingramcontent.com/pod-product-compliance
Lightning Source LLC
Chambersburg PA
CBHW072347200326
41519CB00015B/3693